The Book Within You

The Aspiring Author's Guide

to Bringing the Book Within You, Out

Emily Gowor

Words of Affirmation for Emily

"I knew I felt called to write a book, but I had no idea what to say or where to start – I was stuck. In our coaching, Emily weaved her magic to pull my topics out of me into an outline for my book. Because of her coaching and book outline, I wrote 60,000 words in just three weeks! Writing my first book and putting my thoughts on paper changed my life. Emily supported me through the writing and publishing of my book.00020I know she will draw out the best in you through her heart, soul and experience in writing so many of her own books."

Deborah Toussaint, Author of Ignite Your Life

"Emily is an inspiring book mentor. She helps me look at my writing in a different light, turning my book from a good idea into an incredible experience for myself and my readers. Her advice and guidance on my writing has been invaluable. She is a joy to work with – an asset for any budding author to help perfect a masterpiece!"

Jenni Reiffel, Entrepreneur & Author

"After having been in the very left-brain engineering profession for more than 20 years, I made the decision to leave and pursue a career in the personal development space. Part of my plan included writing a book. Emily was highly recommended, so I took up her services. The first great thing about this was that it forced me to write a synopsis of my book so that I had something to talk with her about. But what has been the most useful aspect of Emily's mentoring has been the coaching.

She is an incredibly wise and insightful young woman with more personal development experience and knowledge than most people twice her age. She has really boosted my confidence and provided reassurance when I have had doubts or been struggling with procrastination. I would not hesitate to use Emily's mentoring again if (and when!) I start on a second book."

Haley Jones, Speaker & Coach

"(I met Emily about a year ago and we immediately clicked.) At some point I decided that writing a book would be a great idea to build credibility and help me secure more speaking engagements, but I wasn't excited about writing the book at all. I spoke to a few book mentors and although they all had systems you could use, I felt that the 'heart' for the project was missing and that I would just be another number. Emily changed all that!

You can feel her passion for books, writing and the whole publishing process – here's someone who lives and breathes books daily. She ignited my passion for writing the book during one short session of brainstorming and opened the floodgates with more ideas, quirky stand-out titles and she just 'got me'! I was completely blown away by her passion and the ease of working with her. She takes all the hassles out of writing a book and makes it a fun roller-coaster ride where you can't wait to get started!"

Alicia Menkveld, Founder of Say YES More Often

"Thank you, Emily Gowor. Without your help, my inspirational journey would never have seen the light of day and, if it did, it would have just been another banged out book in the marketplace. With your help, it put more meaning behind my book by focusing on the detail. You not only brought my book alive but every reader that has read it is absolutely loving it. I'm getting good feedback. People are thanking me for helping them change their perspective on life. I've sold it to all states of Australia and in the USA and the UK, too."

Lance Garbutt, Author of My Never-Ending Journey of Life

"With Emily's coaching, I wrote over 36,000 words in under 120 hours and created a revolutionary, thorough and science-based detoxification program. I am so grateful to you beautiful Emily, like a STAR that shone into a darkened room you have pierced through and switched on the creative juices within. I could not have achieved this without your inspired guidance. Thank you!"

Claudia Carmen Anton, ND

"Working with Emily 1-on-1 took me from disjointed writer to author within a matter of months. Her guidance, her methods, and her inspiration are invaluable tools to anyone wanting to maximise their inner creativity."

Simon Clark, Author of Shift Your View

First published in Australia 2014 by Gowor International Publishing

Revised in 2018

www.goworinternationalpublishing.com

ISBN 978-0-9923493-8-7

Dedicated to my mother, for reading to me for over 400 hours during her pregnancy with me, so that I would be forever be instilled with a deep and great love of words, and to my father, for recognizing my writing talent before I even knew it existed.

TABLE OF CONTENTS

The Aspiring Author   1

Chapter 1: The Book Within, Is Within You   11

Chapter 2: The Art of the Best-Seller   37

Chapter 3: Using the Power of Vision   65

Chapter 4: The 5 Step Process of Book Creation   79

Chapter 5: What's Your Author Style?   117

Chapter 6: Getting into the Writing Zone   123

Chapter 7: The Writers Toolkit   135

Chapter 8: Winning the War on Writer's Block   147

Chapter 9: The Art of Channelling   157

Chapter 10: Turning Life Adversities Into Written Legacies 167

Chapter 11: Mindset = Manuscript   181

Chapter 12: Titles, Subtitles, Covers and More   191

Chapter 13: FAQ's   209

The Published Author   219

The Author's Credo   225

Acknowledgments   227

About The Author

The Aspiring Author

"We write to taste life twice, in the moment and in retrospect."

Anais Nin

For as long as I can remember, I have wanted to put words on paper. Throughout my life, I have had a burning desire to express myself and to let what is inside me, out. In fact, my mother once told me that as soon as I could hold a crayon in my hand, I was writing on the walls of the house! I can't explain it in any other way than writing has felt important – essential, even – for the fulfilment of my life and beyond that, my destiny. Maybe you feel the same way. Maybe you feel you have a message that is asking to be expressed or a story lingering inside your heart waiting to be told. Or perhaps you are filled with information and knowledge that you know can change people lives or businesses, which, in turn, could change the world. *The Book Within You* will help you to follow that feeling, publish a book, and fulfil your dream of becoming an author.

This book will take you on a journey of bringing the book within you, out. It is the aspiring author's guide to achieving this goal. It is informative and profound. It will teach you, solve problems for you, challenge you, and awaken you in the best of ways. It will stir you to ask significant questions and connect with who you truly are. Everything I have included in this book has been drawn from my experience in the art of book writing and how to become an author. It is my intention that by the time you finish reading this book, your relationship between yourself and the page is stronger than ever.

I wrote this book for two types of aspiring authors. Firstly, I wrote it for the entrepreneur who wants to raise their credibility in the marketplace by publishing a book about their topic or niche. And secondly, I wrote it for the creative: the writer who longs to pour their heart and soul out onto the pages of a book (or indeed, several books). Regardless of which one you are (and you may be both), this book promises to help you to write your book.

Revealing decades of personal experience and more than ten years of professional track-record working in the space of books, eBooks, articles, professional bios and more, *The Book Within You* will be your companion on the road to becoming an author. You will learn content I teach to my private clients and find practical solutions to the many challenges authors face in bringing their book to life. It is my intention that this book will inspire and support you to enjoy the experience of writing your book by realizing that creating your manuscript does not have to be a struggle or just another item on your to-do list. In fact, it can be one of the greatest journeys you ever take.

How the Book Within You Came Out of Me

I love to write, and so it seemed natural for me to create my profession around it, and not just because I enjoy it, but because I believe that we help people the most when we are doing what we love. I started out as a professional writer in 2007. It was a journey that led me to write for magazines, produce hundreds of professional bios, and work with incredible individuals to help them bring their content onto the page. I was blessed to work with several leaders, including Dr. John Demartini as I became one of the editors for his best-selling book with Hay House, *Inspired Destiny: Living a Fulfilling and Purposeful Life*.

My desire to write and publish my own writing grew over the years, which has now led to more than nine published books along with a long line of other content including articles, blogs and eBooks. From the moment my first book hit print, people began asking me how I had achieved my goal. They were curious to know what I had done to bring my message to life on the page. It was then that I became a book mentor, coaching and training people around the world to write. The first time I mentored someone and helped them articulate their thoughts and feelings on paper, I loved it so much that I wondered why I hadn't been doing it all along. Speaking on stages and running trainings both on and offline followed and I soon became known for my mission to bring books to life.

I deeply believe in people's potential to achieve their goal of becoming a published author. I believe that people can tick 'write a book' off their list of aspirations if they have the right guidance, which this book endeavours to provide for you. I believe that we don't just have one book within us, but that we have years of wisdom worth sharing. It's been said before that if you don't stand for something, you'll fall for anything. I believe this is true and so it is part of my mission in life to assist people to stand for what they believe is important by writing a book. And that, is how this book, *The Book Within You*, came to be.

The Dream, The Desire and The Gift

Over the years, many people have commented that I have a gift with the English language. It is self-evident that words are my art form (hence why my personal brand remained as the Word Artist for several years from 2009 onwards), and true that I am more confident than some when putting pen to paper. I have no doubt that part of my skill as a writer is because I have a 'gift', which people have referred to over the years. This has led me to ask the following questions when helping other people to write:

Does every person really have what it takes to become an author?

Does every person have the capacity to write a book?

Is there something that writers have that others simply don't?

And finally (and this is the best by far),

How can I awaken the writing gift in other people?

These are deep questions – and perhaps you have asked them, too. Maybe you have looked at people who you think are 'better' at writing than you and wondered the same thing: whether you have what it takes to write a book or whether you too have a writing gift buried inside you. Maybe you have wondered if there is a special DNA that writers are born with that allows them to pour their thoughts and feelings onto the page. And maybe, like me, you may have wondered if there is something different about writers that moves them bring words to the world.

I don't believe that every person is destined to write a book, which is why not everyone does. But, this doesn't by any means imply that we don't all have the capacity for it. If there is even a tiny part of someone that would love to write a book, that is the only confirmation I need in order to know that they do have a writing gift somewhere within them: it just needs to be woken up. Now, you may have absolutely no desire at all to produce words on paper. I have met many people over the years who feel this way. You could argue that these people *don't* have a writing gift. Or, perhaps they do but they have chosen not to use it.

It could be said that I lack a gift as an athlete. Or, it could be said that I simply have no desire to be one and therefore, I will likely never tap into that gift... if, indeed, I do have one. It occurs to me then, that the desire to achieve a goal is the key to finding out if there is a gift hiding inside of us that we haven't unleashed yet – like a writing gift. If you don't dream of writing a book, your heart isn't in it. Simple. But if you are dreaming of it and you can't stop thinking about it, then your heart is in it and you are ready to begin writing or at least work on your book idea!

Studying human behaviour has also taught me that we are often the most talented in the areas that we love most: they are commonly synonymous. I haven't met someone who was extremely talented at something who didn't enjoy it. We tend to bring our talents out and put them on show in the areas we care about most. If you care about writing a book, it tells me there is potential sitting there: raw potential just waiting to be discovered, expressed, and brought out onto the page. And, if you have the dream to write a book but don't end up doing it, then yes, I believe you're leaving potential on the table. I believe that we all have a message to share... and that includes you.

Writing is incredibly powerful and one-hundred-percent free. Anyone can do it. Writing a book can be tough at times: I get that. I've experienced the challenge of capturing my heart and soul on the page more times than you can probably imagine. I have worked for hours to solve a problem in a chapter and get it 'just right'. It's challenging, but the reward far outweighs the pain. In my mind, it's a couple of hours of frustration up against the lifelong sense of achievement you feel after the book is published. In fact, they don't even compare. So, remember as we begin the journey of bringing the book within you, out, that whatever obstacle you are facing now is just a moment in time, but the gratitude you will receive from people and the difference you can make in the lives of thousands of people once the book is written, will last forever.

If you could find a way to overcome every tough moment along the journey to becoming an author, you would soon realize that the effort required is nothing but a tiny blip: that's what I'm here to help you with. Every challenge we face when creating a book manuscript helps us become the author of our own destiny. We must not be afraid to be bigger than the book we are writing, because it's not bigger than us. The book is an extraordinary expression of you and YOU are greatness personified. So, summon the willingness and courage to overcome any obstacle you encounter along the way. Be precocious, persistent, determined. Understand that writing is a vehicle for communicating what's inside your heart with people. Work with it, not against it. You don't need to doubt whether you've got it in you to write an inspiring book that helps people: you do. Instead, focus on bringing the magic within you out onto the page.

I do believe that you can develop your writing gift. I see it in my clients frequently. They start out as tentative writers. As they begin writing, I help them identify their strengths. Over time, they recognize them too. They soon discover there is far more to them than they first realized. Each writer has a different gift. Some are exceptionally talented at humorous writing. Other writers are skilled at presenting facts and information in a coherent and interesting way. Some are gifted at deeply moving the reader into a state of deep contemplation, personal breakthrough, or to tears of realization.

And so, I believe that this question of whether or not you're capable of writing a book is the wrong question to ask if you want to tap into your writing genius.

I believe that it's time to start asking not if you have a writing gift, but instead, what kind of writing gift you have. Are you an academic writer? Are you a story-teller? Are you a poet? Are you a descriptive romantic writer? Are you talented with non-fiction, fiction, first person, third person, factual, surreal, imaginary? Writing gifts shine in many forms and no two people express their gift in exactly the same way. We are all unique and the way that we use our words is no exception to this. You can find your gift and develop it. That's why the greatest dancers never stop training. They just keep dancing. All you need is the flame within you that says, "I dream of this." All you need to start waking up your writing gift is the dream, the desire, and the persistence to get started.

Here are five signs that it is time to start your book:

1. You have a mind full of ideas, thoughts and content

2. You share the same knowledge or life story over and over again with the people in your life: whether they are clients, friends, family and the world around you (social media)

3. You want to leave a legacy (something for the world to know you by)

4. People keep saying, "You should write a book."

5. You have the overwhelming urge to do it (you might be surprised how many people experience this but don't act on it)

Reflect on how you personally relate to each one of these five signs and embrace them as they are the first signs that there is a book within you that is waiting for you to bring it out.

'Banging Out' A Book

Writing a book has become increasingly popular in recent years. You could even say a movement has spread across the world. Business experts around the world are coaching their clients on how important it is to publish your content and ideas into a book to improve your chance of success in life. I celebrate this movement. It has turned the aspiration of writing a book, which was once within reach only to the minority, into an achievable goal for the anyone with the desire to do it. It has turned the overwhelming task of becoming an author into step-by-step systems and helped millions of people to achieve their goal. It has empowered people to speak up about their message.

Having said this, I want to bring your attention to the downside of the movement which is simply this: many people around the world are 'banging out' a book for the sake of saying they've done it or because they're desperate for money and hoping the book will solve their problems in business. This approach has resulted in the production of thousands of low-quality books that have been poorly written and produced – put together without much consideration for the longevity of the book – which can reduce the power that becoming an author has. The book can have a negative effect on the brand, public image, or business of the author, as people do notice when a book wasn't well-produced or cared about. And so, it really does work to your advantage to do more than just 'bang out' a book and to invest the time and attention necessary to produce a piece you can be proud of.

Many books are now produced to be nothing more than a business card on steroids – a fancy brochure for someone's products and services – and so the heart, depth, and soul is often missed in the writing and publishing process. The added danger in this when it comes to increasing your sales in business is that the readers can sense the book was produced purely for income purposes. This can give them reason to doubt your congruency with your message, whether you are just in it for the money, and whether you care about what you do. Ensuring you are 100% satisfied with the product you release into the world will guarantee that becoming an author doesn't backfire on you because the book you published was subpar.

None of the greatest books in history were produced in a hurry. Think of the likes of Plato, Aristotle, Simone de Beauvoir and Ralph Waldo Emerson. While studying philosophy at University, I read some mind-bendingly complex and unbelievable works from these greats and many others. And during my long hours of study, it was easy to see that not one of their works was written in a rush for the sake of making a quick dollar. These greats were deep thinkers and it was because they paid so much attention to the finer detail of their books that their works have long outlasted their bodies and their influence is still felt in the world today. They were focused on producing a masterpiece because they knew that was the only way they and their writing could make a meaningful and lasting impact on the world.

It's up to you to choose what level you play on in becoming a published author. It helps to know what you are aiming for before you even begin. You do have the capacity to be a Plato or a Ralph Waldo Emerson, and the book that you write may very well outlive you, too (I hope it does). It all depends on your vision for yourself as an author and how far you would love your book to go. I would love to invite you to think bigger and aim higher. The difference in time frame to produce a lower and higher quality book may only be a matter of hours, days or a few weeks at the most; which, in the context of your life, is a tiny speck. So, how are you going to approach your book project? I suggest you write it because you are interested in making a difference in the lives of people, first and foremost. If those people are moved by who you are and what you have shared in your book, they will surely reach out and ask to work with you.

I know that many of the world's best writers are hiding under rocks today. I also know that many of the greatest minds will pass away with their knowledge and story still inside them. I first started writing for my personal benefit and soon after that, enjoyment. I wanted an outlet for my feelings: a way to organize my thoughts and grasp the deeper meaning of life. But, as my destiny unfolded, my writing was drawn out into the spotlight and then my entire life changed. The same can happen for you.

I wrote this book to reach out to these writers: to reach out to you. I know that you are hiding away somewhere, either writing or thinking about writing, and that you may be stuck on what to do next to make your dream to of writing a book come true. I know you might not feel confident in your ability yet. I know that you worry about whether your writing is good enough. I know that you might not know what your strengths are as a writer yet. I know that you may feel insignificant in comparison to the bright, shiny best-selling authors who have sold millions of books. I know that you might be afraid of bearing your soul for others to read. And, I know that you might be worried about whether you have enough content to fill a book or concerned that no one will understand you. I have experienced every single one of these concerns over the many years of honouring my own calling to put words on paper and I am here to inspire and empower you to overcome them so that you can finally achieve your dream.

May *The Book Within You* truly be your guide to bringing the book within you, out. I look forward to hearing about your book soon!

Chapter 1:
The Book Within, Is Within You

"Close the door. Write with no one looking over your shoulder. Don't try to figure out what other people want to hear from you; figure out what you have to say. It's the one and only thing you have to offer."

Barbara Kingsolver

The best place to begin your journey to become an author is to understand that the book that is within you, is within *you*. You might be thinking, 'Well, obviously!' Let me explain. As I shared in the introduction of the book, there is an increasing amount of talk in business development arenas about the power of becoming a published author, and therefore, the importance of writing a book to stand out in the marketplace and take your business to the next level. It's likely that you already see how you can increase your professional status, credibility and position in your industry by sharing your expertise on paper. In fact, it may have been the reason you picked this book up. While this advice is valuable (many authors have received greater opportunities once they became published) there is a downside to it that goes beyond moving people to become an author.

By being told that we 'should' write a book, that we 'have' to write a book, or that we 'need' to write a book to help ourselves professionally, we then expect ourselves to do it. But, because in many cases aspiring authors haven't connected with a strong enough reason to write the book – to the point where they would do whatever it took to make it happen – they soon struggle. And then, they beat themselves up when they fail to finish the book (or start it to begin with). It is largely because of this that there are so many unfinished manuscripts laying around on desktops of laptops and computers: because the author wasn't interested in the reality of writing a book beyond it being the right thing to do to grow a business. And because of this, the author lacks the persistence they need to complete the project. Therefore, it goes without saying that in order to ensure that you achieve your goal, you must connect the book you are writing to what is *within* you. You must *feel* it from within. You must *want* to write the book. You must *desire* to write the book.

When a deep desire to write a book is present, amazing feats can be achieved. A desire like this can see you bounding out of bed in the morning and creating an entire outline for a book or writing five chapters in one sitting. Or, it can lead you to do what I did with my fourth book, *The Inspirational Messenger* (which I will share later on): write 51,000 words in 96 hours. In order to initiate a powerful and productive experience of book writing like this for yourself, it's essential that you begin to connect with the book you are about to write, understanding that the book within you, is within you. It's not something that someone else can tell you how to write. It has to come from within. You will be required to care about it, and when it truly comes from within you, caring will come naturally.

I didn't start writing because I wanted to be famous or highly accomplished. I fell in love with words long before anyone knew who I was or that I loved to write. I used to say that I could feel my feelings and thoughts becoming part of the ink in my pen before flowing out onto the page. For me, it was like alchemy: a transformation of what was 'in here' to what was 'out there. And, for most of my writing journey so far, I have remained closely connected with my intimate inspiration to express myself on paper. Find this within yourself. Start there. There is so much more to the experience of becoming an author than status and profit. As you read through this chapter, I encourage you to explore the full extent of what writing a book can do for you, because the phenomenon that occurs between writer and written words is extraordinary and powerful.

To help and guide you to find your 'why' to become an author (where writing becomes like second nature), I first want to resolve a concern that might be playing on your mind and preventing you from starting your book. This concern relates to whether you have enough content for a book, and if you do, what is it? Let's explore the areas you can draw on for your content.

Ideas for Your Content

Answering the question of whether everyone really does have a book within them comes down to, I believe, a question that is far more specific – and makes more sense. And that question is this:

Does every person have enough content inside them for a book?

What I love about that question is that it becomes almost impossible to answer 'No' to it. I believe that a five year old has enough content for a book, so if you are older than five, you will have the same knowledge multiplied by God-knows how many years. Your attention would better be invested into discovering your big why for writing a book; and connecting with your personal drive to write one. Put your doubts about whether you have information and stories to share aside and start thinking about how you are going to do that (which, of course, this book is designed to help with).

For the sake of assisting you as best I can, I have included the upcoming section in the book to point out some of the many places where you might locate your library and wealth of content for a book (or dare I say, books). As you read through this list, reflect on each one. Look through the years of your life. It's time to find out where your content is.

- **Professional experience**

  The content you share in the pages of your book could be filed by your extensive experience of working in a field or profession. Delivering the same service for years or developing your insights in a niche can generate incredibly deep knowledge, or even give rise to a ground-breaking methodology for that industry.

- **Your personal life stories**

  I often connect with people who have been experienced and overcome extreme adversities and tough situations in their lives. Their books have become a place to share their journey. Personal life journeys are a rich source of content for books that could fill volumes if written about in detail. Your own life holds the key to a lifetime of writing.

- **Systems and methods**

  It's entirely possible to devote an entire book to the presentation and explanation of a system or method. Dr. John Demartini's *The Breakthrough Experience®* is an example of this, as it shares the foundation principles for his method, *The Demartini Method®*, as well as detailing the method itself. Regardless of whether your method or system is related to business, relationships, spirituality or another area of life, a book is an exceptional way to solidify and share it.

- **Discoveries**

  Thousands of books have been published over the years containing the findings or discoveries of one or many individuals. Books of this nature are sometimes a journey of discovery about a certain topic (much like my 1st book, *Transformational Leaders* where I interviewed 13 leaders on a quest to understand true leadership) and sometimes the chance for the author to make statements or draw conclusions about research they completed before writing the book.

- **Facts or Knowledge**

  You would be surprised if you knew how much you know. You might choose to reflect on the areas of knowledge that you have and devote your book to sharing it. My advice would be to choose topics of knowledge that you are most interested in and also the ones that, if you published a work on them, would assist you in achieving your goals in life.

- **Philosophies**

  I believe that philosophy and philosophical writings are largely underrated and overlooked in the modern times. I personally love books that were designed to make me think. You may be a deep thinker, and if you are, I am sure that you could produce an incredible book about your philosophical ponderings that would and could change lives. Don't underestimate the power of your own thoughts, ideas and perspectives.

- **A Dream, Message or Vision**

  The book titled *One* by Masami Sato is a beautiful piece that demonstrates how you can turn your heartfelt message, dream or vision for humanity into a published work. If you see a greater future for humanity, write a book about it. If you have a vision for health and wellbeing that could enlighten the world, share it. If you have discovered a core message about relationships that could save marriages, document it. Your dreams, messages and visions are an inspiring source of content.

Now that you have read the above, take a moment now to list out the areas, topics, experiences, stories and knowledge on which you could write about in part of or a whole book. List them out freely. Don't judge them or yourself and don't stop until you have exhausted all of the possible areas of content that you have. What could you write a book about?

_____

_____

_____

_____

_____

_____

_____

_____

_____

_____

_____

_____

Now circle or highlight the ones that you are most likely to write about (think in terms of your life and business goals) and would love to write about. Start to think about the genre of your book and where it would be placed in a bookstore. It is the time to find the goldmine that is sitting in your life right now... just waiting to be turned into words and wealth. Every person is brilliant. Whether they take the time to find and share it that determines to what level they excel in life. Albert Einstein has often been quoted for the following phrase, which reflects this beautifully: "Everybody is a genius. But if you judge a fish by its ability to climb a tree, it will spend its life believing that it is stupid." Your heart, mind and life are literally filled with content to write about. It's within what you have learned, where you have been, who you have met, what you have achieved, and how you felt about all of the above. It's within YOU. It's time to bring it out so the world can benefit from it.

What Is Your Reason for Becoming an Author?

People write books for a variety of different reasons. It's time to connect with yours. Let's become personally acquainted with what your deep, moving drive to complete a book is. Here are the eight incentives people tend to have for becoming an author.

1. Increasing Your Income

Let's start out with a popular reason for becoming an author: money. Many people publish a book because they would love to create another income source or grow their existing one. At the very least, they want to break even on the cost of writing and publishing the book. If generating profit is your top priority as an author, that is perfectly acceptable; however, I encourage you to devote ample time and effort into your marketing strategies to help you turn this into a reality, as not everyone has a life path like J.K. Rowling, Elizabeth Gilbert or Dan Brown when it comes to generating a fortune through book sales alone.

It is important to clarify the numbers you are aiming for in terms of income and revenue. Is it $1000's? $10,000's? Or more? Be clear on this as you start your book. Then focus on creating the plan to manifest that outcome. I wouldn't ever plan on the profits from a book replacing my other sources of my income completely. I suggest diversifying your income sources so that your bases are covered at all times without relying on your book to turn you into a millionaire (which rarely happens).

2. Share a Message

We now move into the second primary incentive for being an author: to share a message. A book is an undeniably effective instrument to play when it comes to singing your song in the world. Oh, the bliss of an infinite number of pages to write upon! The message could go anywhere. And once it's written, documented, bound and published, it can be handed to people like a neat parcel, ready for them to read and enjoy. Yes, sharing a message is definitely a strong incentive for writing a book.

It is the strong belief that this one message can make a meaningful difference to someone's life. For example, that being beautiful isn't always about external appearance. Or, that life is more fulfilling when we manage and move past our fears. Whatever the message is, let me say that there is a place in this world for it. If you are in doubt, take a look in the world around you at all the people whose lives would be more fulfilling or who would be better equipped to achieve their goals if they read your message.

3. Self-Expression

The third primary incentive to become an author is self-expression. This might manifest in the form of sharing your life story as a memoir. It might also show up as producing a book packed full of information that you can't wait to share with your readers. Regardless of whether it's fiction or non-fiction and irrespective of genre, any book can be written from a simple desire to express oneself. I relate to this one, as at least half of my published books were written for self-expression purposes.

The desire to express yourself in a book is not always closely tied in with the desire to generate profits as an author through book sales and further services and products that are offered to the reader. This can often lead to a book that you might call a "best-kept secret". I have no doubt that some of the world's greatest writings are hiding in the 'Documents' folders of hermits around the globe, yet (or never) to be brought out into the light for people to read. Perhaps you have compiled writings like this on your own computer: writing that began because you needed an outlet and finished once you had said what you wanted to say. If you are a self-expression writer, I would encourage you to take your writing further and bring it into a book; because the reward of that self-expression will benefit you for life.

4. Greater Reach, Greater Impact

The fourth primary incentive for people to write and publish a book is to gain broader reach and make a greater impact. This incentive is one that I have found most commonly amongst the world of business. Entrepreneurs, life coaches and speakers from all over the planet want to publish their message so they can become well-known and, as a side-effect, have more people in their trainings and coaching programs. This is an inspiring reason to write a book, with the appropriate level of and an effective approach to marketing, your published title can definitely help you to achieve this outcome.

What to keep in mind here is to be clear on what you will do once you achieve the greater reach – whatever you define that to be. What will you do when your book touches 1000 people? 10,000? 100,000? 1,000,000? Would you love to boost the numbers in your workshops and trainings? Is the reach so that when you release books 2, 3, 4 and 5, that you have an established following of readers? The principle behind these questions is a) to make sure that you are clear and know what you are aiming for, and b) to ensure you have the business systems and sales funnels in place to handle the reach once you achieve it. You don't want all of your hard work to go to waste by touching 10,000 people and having it stop at the book itself. There are literally hundreds of thousands of dollars of business beyond your published piece. Look to the mission beyond having greater reach, or in other words, what having the greater reach allows you to be, do, and have in the future.

5. "Author" Is in "Authority"

Incentive number five for publishing a book is about becoming or being seen as an authority on a specific topic or in a particular field. It's been said many times that becoming a published author gives you added credibility and helps people to see you as an expert. People tend to have respect for someone who has taken the time to organize their information, knowledge, and story in a book that has been intelligently written and well thought-out. This was certainly part of my intention to write *The Book Within You*. By publishing my knowledge on becoming an author, I knew that doing so would assist me to achieve the positioning I was after; to be looked upon as a go-to woman on the topic of writing books. And, of course, this positioning allows me to serve more people, and help them to bring the books within them, out onto the page.

6. Leave a Legacy

The next incentive to become an author is to create a legacy that outlives you. It can be said that many books last a long time and that their pages will often die long after our bodies do. Think now to the great encyclopaedias, the great texts, and the writings of the most well-known, world-renowned philosophers, scientists and thinkers. Published writings certainly have the power to stand the test of time and to cast an influence over generations and centuries to come. And, there is absolutely no reason why you can't produce a book of the same nature: a book that leaves a legacy.

Writing a book to leave a legacy may be as simple as telling your story so that your children and grandchildren will have something to remember you by; so that, when they are adults, they will have the chance to get to know you. Or, writing your book in the pursuit of a legacy might also be about touching the lives of millions of people. It all depends on where you are in life, the world, and what your personal values are. I personally would love to produce a text that sits comfortably between Plato and his friends, or at least one that is read by people a hundred years after I die. But, having said this, it also means a lot to me that any family who outlive me (not necessarily my own children as books are my babies) will have access to me through what I have written. The same can be true for you. You CAN leave a legacy with your book.

7. Make a Difference

The next primary incentive to becoming a published author is to make a difference. This is slightly different than the second incentive, which was to share a message. It extends beyond just one message to what difference the entire book can make on someone's life and is more strongly focused on the outcome. It might be a book that delivers a method for spiritual advancement, business development or healing of the body. Or, it might be a book that inspires a global social movement. Whichever it is, the seventh incentive is strongly focused on the lives that can be changed because of and through your book.

It is focused on the person on the other end: the reader. You might want to make a difference in the lives of your clients. You might want to help people who live in countries where you don't run speaking presentations. Or help your friends to solve a problem – or people who are facing the same challenge that you were. Or, you might want to write the book just to be able to give it away (for example, a book for young adults to help them plan their future). Being able to reach out to a reader and influence them in a meaningful way is a great accomplishment. Keep your readers in your mind as you write, and the book will speak to their core.

8. Media Opportunities

The eighth primary incentive for writing and publishing a book is to gain media exposure. This is another inspiring reason for wanting to become an author, as it suggests to me that you already have a mission that is beyond the book itself *and* that you see the book as a vehicle for achieving that mission. Television shows, newspapers, magazines and radio shows do tend to favour a published voice over an unpublished one; just turn on your television to watch the national morning shows over a week and see how many authors and published writers are interviewed. The title of 'author' will help you to become one of these people.

Now that you have read through what I have observed to be the eight primary reasons for becoming an author, I encourage you to identify which one or ones resonated the most with you. Do this by ticking the top three from the boxes below:

❑ Increasing Your Income

❑ Share a Message

❑ Self-Expression

❑ Greater Reach, Greater Impact

❑ "Author" is in "Authority"

❑ Leave A Legacy

❑ Make a Difference

❑ Media Opportunities

You may have already thought of other reasons to write a book while reading this chapter. Jot them down on the lines below:

_____

_____

_____

_____

_____

_____

Once you have connected with your reason for becoming a published author, keep it in the forefront of your mind throughout the writing process and even when the book goes to print. These incentives may inspire or re-inspire you along the way. For example, as I mentioned, *The Book Within You* has an incentive for assisting me to work with many more budding authors. However, I also had the incentive to express myself on a topic I love. I wrote with the desire to share my world of writing with people. I stayed present with this right up until it was in your hands. So, become clear on your meaningful reason to write a book and stay with it throughout the journey as it will pick you up when you feel down and help you keep moving forwards in moments when you doubt yourself.

The Real Reason You Want to Put Pen to Page

It's time to dive deeper into the reason you want to write a book. This is now about going beyond the eight primary reasons and finding your unique, one-of-a-kind 'why' for writing a book. By placing a deeper meaning on the book itself, you will have all the inspiration you need from the moment you begin writing to the moment you hold the book in your hands for the first time. The following two questions will assist you to find your inspiration to write:

"Why is writing this book so important to me? To my business? To my life?"

and

*"How does writing this book help me go to where
I want to go and be who I want to be?"*

It might help you to find your 'why' if I share what my own personal reason to write is. By baring my soul, it will assist you in bearing yours. The reason I write began when I was a little girl. I would write diaries at home every day and, at school, I wrote fiction books about animals having adventures. Although I don't recall exactly what drove my writing in childhood, I suspect it might have had something to do with the fact that I wanted more friends than I had, and so writing about the animals becoming friends and going on holidays was certainly one way to fulfil that desire. My imagination certainly saved me in many ways as I had few friends throughout my school years.

My reason to write deepened in my early teenage years. I was challenged during high school (who wasn't?) and I needed an outlet for my emotions. I didn't feel that many people understood me, and so the paper became my friend. In the year I was 14, I wrote over 170 poems and a non-fiction book titled *December's Child* (can you guess which month I born in?) My writing didn't judge, mock or criticize me. It gave me the chance to speak up and say what I wanted and express what I both wanted and needed to. It gave me a sense of freedom and relief in times when I felt I had none. It provided me with a private space where I could be alone with my thoughts. I could be myself when I wrote.

Over the years, I started sharing my writing with other people. I wanted to know that I wasn't alone, which, as it turned out, I wasn't. As I grew into young adulthood, I continued to write to help myself through challenges. I shifted from writing pour-my-heart-out pieces to producing self-development pieces which sounded like a pep-talk. I created affirmations which I included in my uplifting prose. My desire to bring so much lightness into my life was largely due to the fact that I was 17, living out of home and finishing high school independently. My parents had divorced earlier that year after two decades of marriage. I was desperately trying to move past it all and think about the future, just so I could get through the day. My writing paid off, as I finished my final year of school with a grade of 96%. In fact, the more I explored the power of self-growth – both my own writing and through the books I read – the better my grades became.

As I left University in 2006 and began my business as a professional writer, my writing became a source of income. As I worked for entrepreneurs around the world, I could sense my words were also the gateway to something greater. And so, during that phase of my life, my writing a business-building, dream-manifesting exercise. Through several years of writing for others, I grew and developed enormously both as an entrepreneur and young woman. Writing became a tool that I could use to achieve two outcomes: one, connect with people around the world, and two, reflecting on what I was learning.

Through my blog, *Life Travels*, I shared my experiences of countries I had been to (as I was also travelling the world at the time) and what I had learned about life while I was there. As it turned out, people loved this style of writing from me, and my blog won a social media award two years running in 2010 and 2011. My inspiration for writing grew stronger as I built a following of thousands of people through my blog, many of who said they felt as though they were on the journey with me.

I discontinued my blogging as I returned to Australia and turned my attention to writing a book instead. This led to the publishing of my first and second books through a publishing house based in New Zealand and Italy. Just over two years later, my third and fourth books, *The Unlikely Entrepreneur* and *The Inspirational Messenger*, were born. As each of the books vary in style – from an interview piece to a semi-memoir to a channelled writing – I fulfilled my desire to push myself to new limits and expand my writing repertoire. I wanted to understand myself more deeply and I wanted to share my story of overcoming depression at age 19 and building an extraordinary life.

Today, my reason to write unites all of these reasons together. I write because I know every time I publish a book, I discover a whole new world that I can share with people. I know that writing peels back our outer layers and shows us who we truly are, and I am inspired to become the greatest version of myself in this lifetime. And I write because I know that my words could unlock a new future for someone. I write because it consolidates my thoughts, feelings and teachings. I write because I become very connected to a higher 'source' when my fingertips touch the keyboard. I write because each book is a new adventure. I write because I know it helps my business and the businesses of others. I write because it is both spiritually-enlightening and professionally-productive. And through all of this, I write because it opens my heart and helps me to truly experience life. I know that there are meaningful opportunities in this world for me, and that publishing books play a role in manifesting those. I know I can live a more fulfilling life by releasing my message into the world.

Ask yourself now, what is your writing connected to: in your life, in yourself, in your future? I suggest answering this question before you begin planning your book. If you don't, you may struggle along the way. The struggle will come simply because we won't know what our content is or where it comes from. We won't know what source it is connected to or where the creativity will come from. We won't be able to access our writing gifts. And, we might not ever finish the book that we've been dreaming of, or working on, for years. And, I believe that you deserve to do just that, and that the world deserves to read it.

Take a moment now to reflect on what your deep reason to write is. Why is it so meaningful to you? What is your deeper calling to write all about? Do you want to be heard? To reach people? Write freely on the lines below.

_____

_____

_____

_____

_____

_____

_____

_____

_____

_____

_____

_____

Take this reason with you in your heart. Let it be your companion on your journey to become an author.

The Author's Journey

Writing a book takes us on a journey as an author: through discovering our reason to write, uncovering our strengths, finding new levels of persistence, and finding out where the book takes us. You can see how writing and the force behind it has supported me through different stages of my life, and how it has been a companion for me since I was a little girl. There were many phases to my journey that have led me to where I am today. Every experience has strengthened my relationship with writing.

Many published authors will tell you that writing the book was an amazing experience and that they grew exponentially as a human being because of it. I agree with the many people who say that it was the journey that made becoming published such a meaningful experience in the first place. One of the exercises I set out for participants in an online training was to write a 2000-

word story about the experience of writing the book once they completed the manuscript. The exercise served a powerful purpose to help them reflect on the journey. They were able to reflect on their growth and transformation. You might choose to do this for yourself when you finish writing your book.

This part of *The Book Within You* is all about becoming acquainted with your Author's Journey. Even if you haven't written anything yet, you have already come a long way on your journey as an author. Up until now, you have been researching for what you are about to write, through either life experience or literal research. Every part of your life to date is an essential component of what is about to come. The book you are about to write only came about because of your past. Reflect on and answer the following questions to begin understanding what your journey as an author has been like up until now, and how it has led you to today.

How long have you wanted to write? Has the desire to write been with you for life?

_____

_____

_____

_____

_____

_____

_____

_____

_____

What role does writing play in your life right now? And, how have you used the written word up until today, across the many aspects of your life, including your professional?

_____

_____

_____

_____

_____

_____

What is your relationship with writing like? Do you resist or embrace it? Do you fight it? Do you love it? Do you live to write or try to avoid it at all costs?

_____

_____

_____

_____

_____

_____

_____

What have you learned about yourself through writing? About the world? About people?

_____

_____

_____

_____

_____

_____

Write openly about your Authors' Journey. Describe the stages, phases, and the twists and turns you have experienced. And then, write about where it has led you to now.

_____

_____

_____

_____

_____

_____

_____

Have you already written books? What else have you written? What was it like? How did each piece turn out? What did you learn from it?

_____

_____

_____

_____

_____

Who are you as an author? What message do you stand for? What style of writing do you have?

_____

_____

_____

_____

_____

By reflecting on your journey so far, you become better equipped to write in the future. Every experience with the pen and page – and every moment where you have thought about writing – contributes to your Author's Journey. It shapes and changes who you are, which in turn, shapes and changes the words that you write. Much like life itself, by understanding the past, we can then create the future.

Overcoming Roadblocks

"Nothing can stop the man with the right mental attitude from achieving his goal; nothing on Earth can help the man with the wrong mental attitude."

Thomas Jefferson

It's time to talk about overcoming roadblocks of writing a book. This later chapters in this book will resolve many of your challenges before you experience them; however, use this section for any other roadblocks you think you may face along the way. The more detail you add while filling out this section, the less likely you are to become stuck while producing your book manuscript. Give it the time as I promise it will be valuable to you. Some of the common roadblocks that first-time authors face (or that you) might face include:

- Getting stuck while planning the book

- Trouble choosing an idea to focus on

- Losing confidence along the way

- Struggling to keep your flow

- Being interrupted while writing

- Not being able to make enough time to write

And many, many others! Reflect on these and answer: what has stopped you from writing a book before now?

_____

_____

_____

_____

_____

_____

What have your biggest challenges been when it comes to writing a book?

_____

_____

_____

_____

_____

What do you think your biggest challenges are going to be in writing your book?

_____

_____

_____

_____

_____

_____

How do you intend to overcome these challenges?

_____

_____

_____

_____

_____

_____

_____

_____

Prepare yourself for the experience of writing your book so you can get the most benefit possible out of it and minimize the time and energy spent on hiccups along the way.

The Power of Intention

Before I sit down to start a new manuscript, I set an intention for the book. I do this for many reasons. The first is that it helps my mind to focus on what I am creating, and it helps me to become present with the journey ahead of me. The second is that I know that I have the power to impact my outcome through intention. So, when I set an intention to, for example, find solutions to each struggle quickly and effectively, I know that my subconscious mind will create exactly this experience. Third, setting intentions is a way of asking for what you want in life. Intentions take your attention off what you don't want and focuses it towards what you desire. In each case, setting an intention has proven to be powerful in helping me to create my end outcome.

What is your intention for yourself as an author?

_____

_____

_____

_____

_____

_____

_____

What is your intention for the book you are writing?

_____

_____

_____

_____

_____

_____

_____

_____

Describe the experience you would love to have while writing your book.

_____

_____

_____

_____

_____

_____

_____

_____

Put your feelings into the intention. Write down what it is that you would really love.

You have well and truly started on your path to becoming an author now. By clarifying the reason you want to write a book, identifying your content, and planning intentions and future solutions to potential roadblocks, you have begun to turn your book from an idea to a reality. This chapter can be used every time you wish you write a book. It focuses on building a strong relationship with yourself as the author and making every effort to work on the same team as yourself. Beating yourself up will slow you down; whereas encouraging yourself to move past the challenges will speed up the writing process and create an outstanding book.

Chapter 2: The Art of the Best-Seller

"My name became a brand, and I'd love to say that was the plan from the start. But the only plan was to keep writing books. And I've stuck to that ever since."

John Grisham

*B*est-selling authors are those who have sold enough copies of their book to a) make it onto a best-seller list in a certain country (e.g. the New York Times Best-Seller List), or b) be the top seller in a selected category on Amazon (e.g. business). Depending on the country you live in, the number of books that must be sold in order to reach a best-seller status will differ, and often by the thousands. In some cases, there are also time frames within which those books must be sold. Naturally, becoming an international best-seller indicates that your book has reached a best-seller status in multiple countries.

The strategies that authors have utilized in order to achieve best-seller status vary, from those who worked with high-end publishers, to those who actively promoted their book through speaking gigs and media exposure, to authors who drove across an entire country on marketing rampage until they achieved their goal. Other authors applied ingenious marketing strategies and leveraged their own databases and professional networks to sell their book by the thousands. I will reveal the qualities of a best-selling book soon, but for now, let me say that regardless of the path the author chose, there were two common factors to these books and their authors:

1. **The book was valuable to the reader** – e.g. it fulfilled a need, solved a problem, or explored a curiosity that thousands, if not millions, of people have/had.

2. **The author believed deeply in the book** – e.g. the author put great effort, heart, and soul into the book.

In order to assist you to increase the chances of becoming a best-selling author, this chapter addresses several components and topics, including exercises. I want to begin by addressing the doubts we experience as writers and how these doubts are actually questions that best-selling authors ask.

The Questions That Make the Difference

Every writers' journey begins with an idea: a concept of a book that they believe the world needs to read or that they want to write. It is an exciting time. It often begins with a dose of nervousness, usually brought about by confronting questions such as "Who will read it?" "Will it be good?" and of course, "What will I think of myself if I don't finish it?" A wise writer will quickly put these concerns to rest, knowing that every problem has a solution.

It is inevitable that you will get stuck somewhere along the way or, shock-horror, that you will want to give up on the book entirely. Do not give up on yourself. Giving up is not an option. There are people who want to read your book as much as you want to write it. You must persist through the obstacles and find the words on the other side. What most to-be authors don't realize, is that the questions they are asking about whether or not they have what it takes to achieve their writing dreams are actually questions that best-selling authors ask. Let me show you how the top three doubts people have (based on my experience so far) are the same concerns that best-selling authors tackle when producing their books, except they don't let it stop them... and neither will you.

1. *"Who Will Buy and Read My Book?"*

I love this doubt that people have for the reason that the explanation for its importance is really quite simple; if you never ask this question, you won't ever be able to craft your plans for the marketing or promotion of the book. In order to market a product or service, you need to know who you are marketing to. The exact same principle applies to books. You can begin focusing on your target readers before you even begin writing the manuscript, and I suggest you do. Do best-selling authors think about who will read their book? Of course! My suggestion is to turn your doubt into a useful question: Who will read your book? Focus on who the book can help; and then work on producing the manuscript, and creative ways to exposure them to the book so they can buy and benefit from it.

2. *"What If My Writing Isn't Good?"*

Worrying that your writing isn't 'good' is a crazy reason to hold yourself back as an author. Is it true that some people are more skilled when it comes to putting their thoughts down on paper? Absolutely. But, I don't tend to believe that there is such a thing as a terrible writer, because everyone can improve. There are many aspects to the art and technicality of writing well, but all of them can be worked on with devotion and the right guidance. Even I never stop improving, and I'm a prolific writer and author. No matter where you are at, take what you have and work on it.

And how is this doubt actually a question that best-selling authors ask? The fact that you are concerned about the quality of your writing says to me that you care whether the readers will understand and enjoy your book. Best-selling authors know their writing needs to embody the qualities of a great book (which I'm about to teach you). They pay attention to how well it reads. Like you, they care whether their writing is "good". So, work on your skills, engage a writing coach, be open to improving your skills, and keep persisting. If all else fails, just know that you don't have to do this alone.

3. *"What If People Call Me A Fraud?"*

Are you afraid your readers will call you a hypocrite or a fraud? This is the third primary doubt that first-time authors face. Regardless of how well your book is written and produced, there will be people who don't like or aren't interested in reading it. There will be people who question the value your book and people who support it. Like in life, it's not possible to please everyone – and it is not wise to try! But, beyond this, if someone is calling you a fraud, it indicates there is something in your book that you weren't comfortable writing: something that you claim to know but didn't know, content you said was yours that wasn't or something you said you do that you don't actually do. The accuracy of the content in a book is also something that best-selling authors concern themselves with, just like you do.

The key to avoiding the scenario where someone attacks you is to stick to what you know. Share from your own personal experience: what you have seen, heard, felt and done. Don't claim to have a degree that you don't have. Teach what you do know. Write from where you are as opposed to lying to the readers about who or where you are and creating an illusion. There is great value to be found within you and your life. If you write the truth, you will lessen the harsh opposition. People won't be able to call you a fraud. And, even if they do, they won't win, and it won't hold for very long... because the truth is the truth and, in the end, only the truth remains.

Now, let's explore what it is that makes a best-selling book, best-selling!

What Makes A Best-Selling Book, Best-Selling?

I frequently have people asking me what it is that makes a book 'good' or 'great'. This might come as a surprise to you, but there isn't one formula or method that answers this question succinctly. Every person on this planet has different preferences for what they like to read and therefore, different definitions of what makes a book 'good'. Some people like books that make them laugh, others like books that teach them something new, and other people like books that move them deeply. Some prefer books that they can immerse themselves in for hours and others prefer books they can flick through while standing at a bus stop.

Based on this, it is impossible to draw one single conclusion about what THE key ingredient to a best-selling book is as it would give preference to certain genres or styles over others. There are, however, general guidelines to consider that will increase the quality of your book and help your core message to come across more powerfully regardless of the style of book you have written; which, I believe, is what defines a 'good' book. The following are what I believe are the top ten qualities of a great or best-selling book:

1. Chronological & Logical Order

The first quality is having the content written in an order that makes sense. In other words, the right content is in the right place. This can be one of the most challenging parts of putting a book together, as we are often so close to our own content that it's difficult to see which idea or concept leads into the next, or which piece come first. Organizing your content in a logical order doesn't necessarily mean every fact and story has to be presented in chronological order. It just means that it is presented in the appropriate place. Point A must lead logically to point B, which must lead to point C, and so on.

2. Smooth Writing Style

The second quality is a smooth writing style. What I mean by this is that the book feels consistent in terms of the tone, tempo, and language within the writing. This can also be referred to as "author's Voice". During the time a book is written, the author may write with five or six different tonalities depending on what they were doing and how they felt on the day they were writing. This occurs more frequently when a book is written over a long period of time: we can encounter many stages of life within even a single year. I suggest extra attention is given to achieve a consistent writing style in these cases. Ensure that your book sounds and feels similar from start to finish so that the readers feel that you are with them 100% of the way.

3. Punctuation & Grammar

I can feel you cringing! Yes, the third quality of a great book is to have clean, organized punctuation and grammar. It enhances the communication between author and reader when punctuation and grammar are correct. Poor punctuation can change or even destroy the original meaning intended by the author. The beauty of this quality is that you, as the author, rarely have to take care of this yourself, as it is primarily the role of an editor to implement proper punctuation and grammar. However, it certainly wouldn't hurt to brush up on some basic punctuation and grammar rules to assist yourself with improving your written communication throughout your life and increase your confidence when it comes to writing your next book!

4. Connection with the Reader

A great book connects with the reader. It is a book where the author thought about the reader when they were typing; which then made the words to leap off the page into the reader's arms. A book that connects with the reader gives them the sensation that the author wrote the book just for them, and they will extract more value and meaning out of the book as a result. The feedback you will get from having this quality present in your book will make the entire effort of producing your book worth it. The more energy you put into the book, the more it will connect with the reader. Stand up for your message. Think about the lives the book will impact. Don't be afraid to speak the reader's language.

5. Originality

I believe every person has an original book within them. And yet, I have read many books that are similar to other books over the years. I personally feel this is because people doubt their ability to share a unique message, or whether they have anything new to say that hasn't already been said before. Because of this, they draw on other people's content to fill in the gaps. While this is fine (provided you reference where appropriate and don't steal someone else's work entirely), I encourage you to persist until you find the one-of-a-kind book that is within you, because the chances of that book flying and becoming a best-seller are significantly heightened. Be you. Be original. There is no one quite like you in this world and you want your book to be a one-of-a-kind just like you are.

6. Flow

A best-selling book flows well from start to finish. This goes beyond making sure that your content is in the right order (the first quality of a great book) to ensuring that the content flows well. A book that flows well leads the reader carefully from chapter to chapter, making sure all the 'gaps' in the book are filled and necessary links have been made. Your book should read smoothly from the first to the last page. This will also increase the level of engagement the reader has with your content. Think about the Harry Potter series by J.K. Rowling as an example of this; thousands of readers around the world struggle to put her books down until they're finished. And then, they hunger for more. Content that doesn't flow gives the reader a chance to put the book down. Re-read your book to see if every paragraph fits together neatly. Every moment you spend checking over your manuscript will benefit you later on.

7. One Main Message or Purpose

As authors, we can sometimes be guilty of becoming, well... too excited! We begin writing and then we want to pour everything onto the page. On the plus side, this leads to us discovering just how much content we have inside of us. On the flip side, it can lead to us putting too much content, or content across too many topics, into one book. Great books have one main message or purpose. They keep it simple and straightforward when it comes to the topic, and then they go deep into that one topic. For example, there might be a book on the power of being a woman where all the content within it helps women to realize how beautiful and magnificent they are. Or, the book might be about business development where the author presents a single method on how to develop a thriving business. Both of these books would not only be less confusing to write, but easier to market. Find out what the main message or main purpose of your book is and stick to it. If need be, you can always write two, three or ten books until you have published your extensive repertoire of content!

8. Takes the Reader on a Journey

I believe every book takes the reader on a journey. This applies regardless of genre, type, length, size or style. Fiction novels transport us to alternate worlds.

Self-growth or self-help books take us into a realm of alternate possibilities for life. Business books step us through the development of our businesses, organizations, and entrepreneurial pursuits. Some books, such as The Alchemist by Paulo Coelho, take the reader on a deep journey from start to finish, which in this case, was very much a journey of self-discovery and brilliance.

And so, the eighth quality of a great book is about taking the reader on a journey. View every chapter of your book as a stage in the journey and every page as a step. Reflect on the overall journey that the reader takes from start to finish. What do they discover about themselves? About life? About that topic? Where do they begin and where do they finish? What kind of journey will they go on after they have read the book? The most artful authors in the world are those who consciously craft the journey the reader will go on. You too can do this with your book.

9. Captivating Introduction

A great book also has a captivating introduction. It engages the reader and gives them a compelling reason to read on and finish the book. Without a captivating introduction, you run the risk of losing people who would potentially buy your book, especially as many people flick to the introduction of a book in a bookstore to see if the book is up their alley. You want your introduction to inspire you. I know that I have hit a winner if I find myself feeling deeply moved or inspired when I'm tapping out the first words of my book. Feel as though you are about to deliver a seriously important, profound, highly valuable and even deeply moving message to the reader: like giving an award-winning speech, except in a silent format. Remember, if you are inspired writing the introduction, your readers are going to feel exactly the same way and they are going to feel like, "Oh, this one's going to be a good one" ... and they're right. Because if you are inspired writing your introduction, then it is my guess that the rest of the book is going to follow suit.

10. Adds Value to the Reader

The tenth quality of a great book is that it adds value to the reader. This quality is about sharing your content while also being present with how specifically that content will help the reader in their lives. A book can add value in many ways. A fiction book helps the reader to take some time out of their life to relax. A book on relationships might guide the reader to improve their communication with their partner. Other non-fiction books might assist the reader by presenting information that the reader can use in their businesses or lives. Sharing your life story in a book may uplift others to live a higher quality life.

Regardless of what genre your book is and what topic you have chosen to write about, be clear on the value that your book brings to the lives of your readers. In becoming clear on this, you may even discover marketing angles or lines you can use when you are promoting your book. This may sound obvious, but the more value that your book adds to the reader, the more valuable it will be in the readers' eyes, which will naturally lead to a greater number of book sales as people will recommend it to their friends and clients. Here are a few questions to help you identify how the book you're writing can assist the greater humanity:

Which books are missing from the shelves?

What message does humanity need right now?

What content or story could help the world?

What problems are humanity facing right now?

At the end of the day, you need to be personally inspired by the book you are writing. As Cyril Connolly stated, "Better to write for yourself and have no public than to write for the public and have no self." Apply these ten qualities to your manuscript. Then, identify what you believe makes a best-seller status and don't stop until you are certain your book embodies it.

The Qualities and Beliefs of Best-Selling Authors

From my observation, becoming a best-selling author is as much about the psychology behind it as it is about the achievement itself. Our perspectives and attitudes on life are incredibly potent when it comes to creating an amazing reality. Our mindset determines how we see ourselves and the world and therefore, what we allow ourselves to receive and achieve in life, including whether we reach the status of a legitimate best-selling author. The following points reveal the core qualities and beliefs of best-selling authors.

- **They know they have a message to share that serves people**

  Best-selling authors live with the certainty that they have a message – if not one, many – to share with people. They speak up and stand for that message. They realize they have years of wisdom, life experience and knowledge to bring to the world through the pages of their books. And, they want to share it because they know in their heart that it serves the world.

- **They are willing to show themselves to the world**

  Best-selling authors tend to have less shame about who they are human beings. They know who they are, and they love who they are. They are authentic. And, because of this, they are willing to show themselves to the world. It is our shame on who we think we are or are not that stops us from being exposed to millions of people. The more you appreciate and honour your true self, the more accomplishment will come your way.

- **They feel worthy of their achievement as an author**

  One of the qualities that stands out for me is that many best-selling authors feel worthy of their achievement and worthy of being in the limelight. They know their devotion is worthy of being rewarded financially through income and socially through status. Because they feel worthy, their fears and doubts dissolve... and they succeed. They know they worked hard for it, they believe in their book, and they are willing to receive the accolades that come with that.

- **They are humble about their achievements**

  Best-selling authors generally tend to remain humble about their achievement. When I heard Elizabeth Gilbert speak several years ago, she wasn't focused on the 10 million books she had sold or the money she made from it: she was focused on the message she was delivering to the audience. She is focused on the magic of writing, not only on book sales and status. With the trend on becoming an author growing, we can sometimes become too attached to the ego of becoming a best-selling author as opposed to focusing on the service our book provides. It's about the readers as much as it is about you.

Reflect on yourself in relation to these beliefs and qualities. Do you know what your core message is? Are you comfortable and confident being in the limelight? To what degree do you truly love yourself? Do you feel worthy of selling thousands of books? Are you clear on your mission as an author? Are you setting out to help people? Or, are you doing it solely for the status and fame, so you can look good in front of other people? Observe best-selling authors and begin to embody their beliefs and qualities within yourself.

Bursting the Best-Seller Bubble

There is a common misconception that becoming an author will solve all of your problems in life. Business owners all over the world are writing and publishing books in the hope that they will suddenly become a best-seller – or a raging success – overnight. While this does happen for a small percentage of people (primarily due to large databases, high level marketing and extensive media exposure), this fantasy can often become a fallen dream for the majority of aspiring authors who put in the hard yards and wind up with 5,000 copies of their book in their garage. Making a book fly takes dedication and a high level of devotion and becoming a published author is about so much more than the product you now hold in your hands.

See, what most people don't know is that it took 24 years for Louise Hay's *You Can Heal Your Life* to become an 'overnight' best-seller. Multiple international best-selling authors like Dr. John Demartini become best-sellers within a matter of days from the date of publish because of the constant effort they put in behind the scenes before the book was even written, let alone published. In fact, what you might not know is that Dr. Demartini does 1000 radio, media and television interviews a year. And so, it's no wonder that he sometimes sells 20,000+ books inside the first week of release. Both of these accomplished individuals are about so much more than just the books that they write: they have a mission beyond it.

In the simplest of terms, becoming a published author is an opportunity to amplify the difference you make in the world. It is an opportunity to share content you are already teaching and stories you tell from stage. And so, the most important thing to make sure of is that, put simply, you have plans *beyond* just publishing the book. A book *adds* to who you are, it doesn't *make* who you are. A book reflects what you do and the value you add to people aside from the book, especially if you are in business or have a personal brand. It helps you to expand what you already do, further. It doesn't stand on its own: it is part of your plan to impact and inspire the world.

The following questions will help you to clarify the difference you are making in the world as well as being a published author. Which services do you provide to the world?

_____

_____

_____

_____

_____

_____

_____

_____

What other products do you sell besides the book?

_____

_____

_____

_____

_____

Which keynote presentations can you do on topics from the book?

_____

_____

_____

_____

What live events can you run on topics from the book?

_____

_____

_____

_____

_____

_____

What business or joint ventures could you establish?

_____

_____

_____

_____

_____

What projects can you be a part of?

_____

_____

_____

_____

_____

Who can you serve?

_____

_____

_____

_____

_____

_____

Who would you love to serve?

_____

_____

_____

_____

_____

What would you love to be famous for?

_____

_____

_____

_____

_____

If you could leave a legacy behind you in the world, what would it be?

_____

_____

_____

_____

_____

_____

The truth here is that you are already 'somebody' before or without even writing a book. Becoming a published author simply amplifies who you are and what you do. So, who do you most want to be? And, more importantly, how would you most love to make a difference? Becoming a published author is an amazing opportunity to be and do just this. You can create an entire movement around a book and body of work (take *The 4-Hour Work Week* by Tim Ferriss, for example). Your book can easily become the backbone upon which you develop a whole business running seminars, courses, online trainings and private coaching with people. It can become the connecting point for your life's work.

A Measure of Success

Before you become a published author, it is important to clarify what your measure of success is going to be. To help you define this for yourself, I will share mine with you. Many times, I have asked myself what my own measure of success as an author is. While being a best-selling author is part of the goal – because, of course, it would be meaningful to achieve it – it's not my sole aim. I measure my success as an author on several other components which are more subjective than book sales alone, despite having sold more than 5,000 copies of my first book, Transformational Leaders. First and foremost, I want to know that I did my best work. I live for the feeling that I have satisfied the creative within me; that part of me that yearns for self-expression. This measure of success relates to me and only me.

My second measure of success is the feedback I receive from people about the book. When people say to me that my books empowered, uplifted and inspired them, I consider it a success. On numerous occasions, people have said my writing saved their lives or helped them to turn a corner in their life. I have also had people say that, after reading my content, they felt they knew me well and could relate to my experiences. I desire for my writing to have a deep and lasting impact on people's lives, and so the number of books sold merely reflects how many people's lives were impacted.

My measure of success as an author is also partially related to how many topics I explore and write about. I am a deep thinker, and the pages are a way for me to pursue my curiosity. I have a personal interest in delivering many messages throughout my existence so that many people can benefit across many topics. This also extends to how many different styles of books I can produce. I am also intrigued by the infinite number of ways a book can be put together, and each one of my books teaches me a new skillset I can share with people. The blend of all of these measures of success makes my pursuits as a writer and author fulfilling.

One of my clients said something magnificent during a session in relation to becoming a best-selling author which is worth sharing. She said, "The divine (the universe, God) already has a plan for where this book is going to go." It was an incredibly empowering thing to say, as it indicated that she wasn't afraid of how far her book might or might not go, regardless of whether it influences a hundred or ten thousand people. She was focused on the message being received by those who need it most. So, while you are likely to want to be a best-seller (which I celebrate) and to achieve credibility (which will happen), it's also wise to keep your attention on the service your book provides. Focus on serving people and craft a masterpiece they will love.

Getting Beyond Your Book

Regardless of what your measure of success is, it's essential to have a reason for becoming a best-selling author that extends beyond book sales and the professional and social status. Both of these will often lack the magnetic power to draw in the right people and opportunities to help you to achieve your goal. Getting beyond your book is about putting your attention on the readers. It's about seeing where the publishing of this book is going to lead you down the line, bearing in mind that the greatest opportunities may not even require you to become a best-seller in order to access them. It's about sensing and knowing which lives will be altered because of what you wrote. Utilize the following questions to help you clarify your personal mission and 'why' to become a best-selling author. Focus on YOU. Focus on THEM (the readers). Stop, become present, open your heart and then write.

Why do you want to become a best-selling author?

_____

_____

_____

_____

_____

_____

_____

_____

What would be so meaningful about this accomplishment? What does it mean to you?

_____

_____

_____

_____

_____

_____

_____

_____

What difference would you love to make to the lives of other people by becoming a best-selling author? What's in it for them?

_____

_____

_____

_____

_____

_____

_____

How can you inspire and uplift people by being a best-selling author? How can you pass on the torch to them?

_____

_____

_____

_____

_____

_____

_____

Once you have filled these out, let's talk about specifics in terms of which countries you would love to impact with your book and how. Use the following world map to highlight the countries or domains in which you would love your book to go. It doesn't matter if you only select one or two – even this is a mission big enough to keep you busy for life!

Now, list out the cities, countries and nations you want to influence with your book in the table below and in the second column, write out how, why and in what way you would love the book to make a difference in that particular location in the world.

City, State, or Country I Would Love to Influence	The Difference I'd Love to Make – What and Why *E.g. educate the population about finance, give the youth hope for a brighter future, empower women in business.*

Before we conclude this section, I want to talk about the financial aspect of becoming a best-selling author. I believe in the profound principle that money and great wealth are drawn to those people who have the biggest, most compelling and heartfelt reasons for it, often reasons that extend past themselves. Answer the following two questions to assist you to find YOUR reason.

What will I do with the income I earn as a best-selling author? How will I use it?

_____

_____

_____

_____

_____

_____

_____

What will I do in and for the world with the money I earn? What will my contribution to the world be?

_____

_____

_____

_____

_____

_____

I value the process of wealth creation as I understand that it allows me to create a ripple effect in the world. The greater my wealth, the greater my impact. It awakens our capacity to be resourceful and to see opportunities where other people don't. It enables us to focus our skills and talents to solve problems in the world. With wealth, you have greater power to impact communities, play in a position of influence and initiate social movements across the world. Wealth can be yours and so can the difference you make with it. And finally, I want you to take a moment to write a mission statement about your why as a best-selling author on the lines below.

It is my mission as a best-selling author to

_____

_____

_____

_____

_____

_____

Upwards and onwards!

To Buy or Not to Buy

You now have a greater awareness about what it might take to reach best-seller status with your book. It will require persistence and long-term quality marketing and media exposure. Since it will take effort, like the greatest accomplishments often do, it makes it even more important to ensure that when your book is exposed to thousands, hundreds of thousands, if not millions of people, that it sells. This section of the book explores this. Let's have a closer look at the different reasons people buy books.

First of all, it has to be said that many people buy books based on its visual appearance. People say, "Don't judge a book by its cover" but we all do. People are more likely to be drawn to and purchase things that look, well... pretty. I am definitely drawn to books based on looks first. I will spot the spine or cover of a book from several metres away in a book store and make my way over to pick it up and hopefully, for the author's sake, buy it.

Now, there is certainly an art to a great book cover (this is covered later in the book) and it's true that not one book cover will appeal to all the potential readers based on varying preferences. But, of course, like in life, it's not your job to please everyone: only the people who are, with certainty, going to be interested in and benefit from your book. Your task is to ensure you pay as much attention to your cover as you do to the inside content. I am sure, that like me, you have neglected to buy books because the cover didn't 'grab' you: perhaps it was due to being the wrong colours, cheap or tacky in appearance, disturbing, offensive, or about a poor fit for the topic of the book. The contents of the actual book may be brilliant, but because of the cover, you (or the reader) never gets to experience it. You don't want this to happen to your book!

The second way I've seen people buy books is through the title and or subtitle of the book. The way a book is named can either draw you in or put you off. I have also picked up books off the shelf to buy them based on their title. An example of this is a book I bought in late 2013 by Rasheed Ogunlaru titled *Soul Trader: Putting the Heart Back into Your Business*. The title was a very clever play on words and it reflected the content of the book beautifully.

Other people will (and this might sound strange if you've never done it) purchase books based on the third way, the Table of Contents (sometimes noted as the TOC). A contact of mine picked up my fourth published book, *The Inspirational Messenger*, and the first thing she did was open up to the TOC. Sitting beside me, she read all of the chapter titles out-loud, murmuring, "Yes, uh huh, yes, good." Was I a tiny bit nervous? Yes! But, thankfully for me, she was impressed and proceeded to buy the book. This reminded me how important chapter titles themselves are in terms of catching interest– but we'll cover this later on.

The fourth way I've watched people buy books is through the content itself. In other words, they do what I call the "flick-through". They open to the inside of the book and read a few paragraphs or several pages to see if the book is for them. In the simplest terms, they're looking to see if that book can help them get more of what they would love in life. They want to know if will be worth their time to read. They want to know if your knowledge is going to provide a return on investment for the thirty-odd dollars they will potentially spend to buy your book. It's a standard process, people do it every day, and they *will* do it to your book.

Now, some people, like myself, do the "quick-flick". I am on the ruthless side when it comes to checking over the content is in a book. I flick to five or six different random pages in the book and make a quick evaluation over how 'good' the content is: in other words, how engaging it is, how well it's written, and whether it is of interest to me. It goes without saying that I am interested in what different authors and publishers have done in bringing books to life as there is always something to learn. However, when I'm shopping for myself, I am extremely picky – and so are your readers.

The fifth main way I've watched people buy books is through the blurb: essentially, the words on the back cover. I would suggest including a blurb on the back cover explaining what the book is about. You might be sitting there thinking, "Don't all books have blurbs?" Well, it's interesting because until recent years, I would have thought so too. But, what surprises me often when I browse through a book store is that a high portion of books don't use a straightforward blurb on the back cover. Instead, they pack it with testimonials and reviews about the book.

This personally frustrates me. Unless it's Bill Gates or Oprah Winfrey writing a personal comment about the book on the back cover, I'm generally not that persuaded nor am I interested in what Joe Smith has to say about the book. I am more than capable of making up my own mind about whether I'm interested in the book and I'd prefer to hear about what the book will do for me than hear someone else I don't know ramble on about it. I would prefer to flip over to the blurb, read it, and feel that the author was speaking directly to me as it creates personal connection. A blurb is informative and direct, and testimonials edify the author to the reader. It's up to you which one you would prefer; however, I personally look for information if I'm buying a book as it helps me to reach my decision quicker.

Now, this isn't to say that testimonials aren't useful in helping your reader make a positive buying choice, because they are. But I would be more inclined to feature them in the online marketing or printed materials about the book or in the front of the book as opposed to on the prime real estate of the back cover which is as important as the front cover. Having said this, as a general rule, one testimonial is usually fine as long as you make it a potent one that isn't too long, and don't sacrifice the opportunity to tell new potential readers about the boo. Play it to your advantage. I will educate you about the art of writing a great blurb for your book later on.

Over the years, I have witnessed every single one of these in action, and I have done them all myself when buying books to read. It's time to examine your own book-buying habits to further the appreciation of how important the many components of your book are.

Why Do YOU Buy?

Take a moment now to think about how you buy books. Answer the following questions by ticking the box you feel fits you best:

- Which of the following elements 'converts' me the *most* into buying a book?

  ❑ Author's Name or Status

  ❑ Author's Previous Books

  ❑ Front Cover

  ❑ Title

  ❑ Subtitle

- ❏ Table of Contents

- ❏ The Content

- ❏ Interior (how it looks)

- ❏ Blurb

- ❏ Back Cover

- ❏ Social Recommendation

- Which part of a book do I consider to be *most* important in making it sell?

  - ❏ Author's Name or Status

  - ❏ Author's Previous Books

  - ❏ Front Cover

  - ❏ Title

  - ❏ Subtitle

  - ❏ Table of Contents

  - ❏ The Content

  - ❏ Interior (how it looks)

  - ❏ Blurb

  - ❏ Back Cover

  - ❏ Social Recommendation

You might reflect on your recent book-purchasing adventures to answer the above questions. Bearing these in mind, it goes to show that you must think about your book on a global scale. You must pay attention to all of the finer details about your book from the cover right through to the contents, not just what you think will make it sell based on your own experience or someone else's. You must think about your target readers as being in the millions. It will hold you to higher standards. In turn, this means that you will hold your book to higher standards and therefore, produce a book that knocks it out of the ball park.

It's important to note here that I don't expect you to crush your creative spirit under the expectation that your book (especially if it's your first one) has to be extraordinary. I know that my first two books felt more like a practice run than the real thing, and that as I continue to write, I have found my feet and watched what happens when these components are "right". You know you have nailed it when one or more (hopefully, all) of the following things occur:

- People ask to represent or on-sell your book through their company – e.g. through their website, office, speaking gigs

- Media opportunities start to present themselves to you without too much effort

- People buy your book based on even one of the components we've talked about so far

- Your book sells itself e.g. people are asking for it instead of you having to promote it

I had an experience recently where I was at my hairdressers. Now, my hairdresser and I have been in a relationship (just kidding: but you know what it's like, you tell your darkest secrets to your hairdresser) for over six years and so, she knows what I do for a profession. A week after *The Inspirational Messenger* was in print, I went in for a regular appointment. While I was there, she asked me about my books. When I mentioned the title of my newest masterpiece, she said, "I'll buy one for my sister, bring one in." She was sold on the title itself and it wasn't even for her. Of course, I did. A few weeks later I received a text message from her telling me how much her sister had enjoyed the book.

Another story which demonstrates this is a great one, from New Year's Day 2013. It was 9:30 a.m. and I had already been wide-awake for nearly three hours working on my business, writing and more: a sign that you are doing what you love. As the clock ticked over to 9:30 a.m., a visitor dropped around for someone who was living in the same house. And as she walked in, she walked by my desk and said, "I think I'm going to have to get another copy of your book." And just like that, I sold a copy. Now, picture this. I was sitting there in my pyjamas. I wasn't hung-over since I don't drink, but I certainly hadn't showered. My hair was a mess, I had no make-up on: you get the picture. This is a small example of what happens when you produce a book you love inside-out. Work through all of the components above to make your book an outstanding one.

When we write a book that we care about and do it well, the world feels it and responds to us accordingly. People stop to pay attention to our books and they will take the time to buy and read it. Some will even make the effort to write to you and share an acknowledgment. Opportunities to gain greater exposure for your book appear and you enjoy the journey of bringing your books to more people. And if and when you hit best-seller status, the accomplishment will mean that much more. So, work on writing an inspiring book, build your profile before publishing it, and open yourself up to great possibilities.

Chapter 3: Using the Power of Vision

"I am the vision. God is the power. Together we're the team."

Affirmation, source: Dr. John Demartini

O ver the years, I have come to appreciate how powerful working and living with a vision is. When we see a vision in our mind, we have hope. We have something to aspire for, something to work towards and something to believe in. This chapter will prepare you to write by helping you to clarify your vision. In it, we will cover two parts: fact and feeling. By working through both sections, you will begin to more fully engage the power that a vision has to help you achieve your goal as an author, both with and beyond the book. You will clarify your vision – and then you will fulfil it.

PART 1: THE FACT

To tap into the inspiring essence of your future as an author, we are going to begin by outlining some of the practical details of your vision: the facts. This will guide you move through your human mind to access the higher nature of your soul: the all-knowing, all-seeing, all-being part of you that, when connected with, brings deep meaning and inspiring purpose to your life. The questions you are about to fill out answers to relate more specifically to the what, when, and where components of your vision. Begin with the details that you have and work from there. There is no reason to fear this exercise as it's entirely possible that you are clearer on your vision than you might think. This process will simply unfold and document that clarity. Once it's down on paper, you will see it so much more clearly. Or, you will see the areas that aren't yet clear, and be able to devote your attention and energy to bringing them into focus.

It's Time to Meet Your Readers

Clarifying who your readers are comes first. In the next chapter, I will assist you to clarify your book idea which you may choose to do before answering these if you're not yet sure what you will be writing. But, if you have at least some idea of what your book is about, complete this section now. Now, you may not know every detail about your readers. You might be sitting there wondering how you're supposed to know anything about them; but you will at least have some sense of who they might be. Start with what you do know about them and work backwards. Focus on the smaller details, but don't be overly caught up in how much detail you are able to extract.

Who are your target readers?

_____

_____

_____

_____

_____

_____

_____

_____

Are they:

- Male

- Female

- Children?

- Teenagers?

- Young adults?

- Middle-aged

- Elderly?

- Any particular nationality?

- Any particular religion?

- Any particular body type (you just never know)?

- Healthy or unwell?

- Employed or unemployed?

- Athletic or passive?

- Intellects or 'feely' people?

Where do they live in the world? Are they even based in your country?

_____

_____

_____

What do they do for a living? What types of careers do they typically have?

_____

_____

_____

_____

_____

What are their likes, hobbies, past-times and interests?

_____

_____

_____

_____

_____

What are their main questions, worries, problems or concerns in life?

_____

_____

_____

_____

_____

What are the core values of your readers? E.g. business achievement, family or spiritual advancement

_____

_____

_____

_____

_____

Who would enjoy this book most?

_____

_____

_____

_____

Who would receive the most benefit out of this book?

_____

_____

_____

_____

_____

If you struggled to answer the above questions, don't worry. I struggled when I was writing my first books too. In fact, it took me awhile to begin thinking beyond the book I wanted to write to the marketplace. It's important to find that perfect balance of writing for you (because you have a message to share) and writing a book that the wider world would love to read.

Business Opportunities

This section of planning your vision is about the business opportunities that you could create or take related to your book. Work through the following questions now.

What is the call-to-action for your reader from your book? What is the next step for them to take with you? E.g. coaching, one day workshop, free trial.

_____

_____

_____

_____

What speaking presentations will you deliver related to your book?

_____

_____

_____

_____

_____

Which seminars or trainings will you run related to your book?

_____

_____

_____

_____

List all of the places you would love to sell your book:

_____

_____

_____

_____

Who do you know that would love to promote your book to their databases?

_____

_____

_____

Who would you love to source video and/or written testimonials for your book from?

_____

_____

_____

Continue developing your business plan around the book as you write it. Remember that it is an ongoing process of development; a work-in-progress; like every business and aspiration.

Media Opportunities

The biggest slip-up new authors make when it comes to achieving media exposure is thinking that they are going in the media to talk about their book. Wrong! You are in the media to share the message and what you do in relation to that message; of which your book is a reflection. This is an essential distinction I received while in a one-day training with Kate Engler, a PR expert in Australia. The book acts as a prop for you to use when you are being interviewed in the media. Media for authors is a huge topic in itself, but I will say that a press release which pitches a headline "Sally Jones Publishes New Book on Relationships" won't typically land well, as it focuses on you not on the message you want to communicate. Lead with the message, and let the book help you to deliver it in the media. It's time to clarify the media exposure you would love to receive as a published author.

Which television shows would you love to appear on as a guest?

_____

_____

_____

_____

Which newspapers would you love to be featured in?

_____

_____

_____

_____

Which radio shows would you love to be interviewed on?

_____

_____

_____

_____

Which magazines would you love to be featured in?

_____

_____

_____

_____

Which online platforms would you love to be featured on?

_____

_____

_____

_____

Gaining media exposure can help you to touch the world with your story and message.

PART 2: THE FEELING

"If a book changes your life by you writing it, it will probably change the lives of the people reading it."

Emily Gowor

The second part of engaging the power of vision in the book writing process is about 'feelings'. This is what you might refer to as mushy stuff, but is equally powerful, if not more, than a list of facts. You might have noticed that having a vision isn't just about the book that you're creating: it's about your life. It's about you. It's about what you ultimately dream of doing, and then how the book assists you to just that.

I envision writing many, many books; because each one marks a different layer of my dream. It unfolds a new level, explores a new domain, and raises the foundation upon which I place myself in the world. Those who live with vision – even one vision – go further and achieve more than those who don't. Those who connect with their highest vision are marked down in the history books as having made a huge difference to humankind and the world. And, those who live with a vision from the heart, write books that linger in the hearts and minds of others for years to come. It's time to unlock your greatest vision. Tune in to your heart as you answer the following questions.

What is your vision for your book?

_____

_____

_____

_____

_____

_____

_____

What transformation would you love your readers to have by reading your book?

_____

_____

_____

_____

What relationships will you form with your readers?

_____

_____

_____

_____

What do you imagine people saying about your book once it's published?

_____

_____

_____

_____

_____

How many people can you envision your book, this book, touching?

_____

_____

_____

_____

Open yourself up to your true desires. Ask your heart to reveal your vision to you.

Now that you have fleshed out both the fact and feeling elements to your vision as an author – and for your book – it's time to bring the two halves together; as every great vision incorporates the two. A truly inspired vision statement blends the facts and the feelings together. *E.g. In my vision as an author, I see my book selling over 10,000 copies to women in the USA to assist them with empowering their financial area of life and achieving their dreams. I believe in the power of every human being to overcome struggle and succeed, and the vision for my book is to assist women to move past financial set-backs and do exactly this.*

Write your vision statement now:

_____

_____

_____

_____

_____

_____

_____

_____

_____

_____

Type up this vision statement and put it somewhere where you can see it daily. And, in every moment where you doubt yourself, reflect on it. Let the clarity of your vision guide you to the fulfilment of your dream: holding your book in your hands for the first time.

As Kobe Yamada said, "Follow your dreams, they know the way." Your inner aspiration and what you see for you and the book in the future have the tremendous ability to bring you everything that you need to finish your book. So, engage with your vision. Work on the facts and feelings of your vision until it enlivens you from your mind to your heart, body and soul. Write for your vision and let your vision guide you to write.

Chapter 4: The 5 Step Process of Book Creation

"By failing to prepare, you are preparing to fail."

Benjamin Franklin

*W*riting a book can feel like a daunting project to take on: I've heard about it several times in the hundreds of people I've talked with about becoming an author. People have asked me how I "did it" and about the approach I took in producing so many books. Having mentored so many people to write, I certainly do have a system I follow when creating manuscripts. This chapter will walk you through it. I call it the *5 Step Process of Book Creation*. It's time to dispel the mystery about what the stages of writing a book are, so that you have a greater chance of achieving your goal of becoming a published author. The following graphic shows the five step process:

CONCEPT STRUCTURE REVIEW EDIT

Just to be clear, these five steps are what must occur *before* your book goes to publish. There are several more that occur after the book is edited, all involved with the actual publishing process. This process will guide you to move from a blank page to an edited manuscript, so that you can move to print and publish. The final step of the process – edit – may or may not be in your hands depending on the publishing option you select for your book. Let's dive into a detailed exploration of the process, staring with Step 1: Concept.

Step 1: Concept

The first step of the book creation process is to decide on your 'concept': in other words, your book idea. This sounds incredibly obvious however there is more to it than saying, "Hey, I should write a book about business" and then going off and doing it without giving it much thought. The book idea is a, if not the, most crucial stage of the process of book creation. This is because the quality and clarity of your book idea can make or break your achievements as an author.

A powerful book idea is a) clear, b) unique and/or original and c) a solution to a reader's problem or an answer to their question. All of these components are established during the idea stage of book writing. If any of these core components aren't in place in the initial stage of choosing a book idea, it can lead to several challenges later on when it comes to marketing and selling the book, including sending the manuscript to potential publishing houses, gaining media opportunities or promoting it to your databases and connections. The last thing you want is for only your close friends and family to buy the book and the rest of the world to say, "Congratulations!" and "I'm so proud of you!" before vanishing without buying the book. You want to have people interested enough in your book to buy and read it. So, ensure that you address all of these elements when you are refining and finalizing your book idea. The following will assist you to do this.

Is It *Clear?*

My golden rule on book ideas is this: if you can't explain it in 15 seconds, it's not clear enough. I've heard too many people over the years struggle when it comes to answering a very simple question: "What is your book about?". It is crucial that you are clear on your book idea, otherwise you won't be clear when explaining it to potential readers, especially when you are marketing the book. Here are five examples of clear versus vague book ideas to give you a guideline to follow when it comes to clarifying your book idea:

Clear Book Idea	Vague Book Idea
A book on how I found God while travelling through India	My journey through India
A book teaching the ten steps to becoming a millionaire	A book about how to build wealth
A book that shares a step-by-step process of overcoming grief and rebuilding your life in three months	A book on overcoming grief
A book on how to help your children find their purpose in life	A book about parenting
A book that reveals one hundred ways to move on from a break-up	A book on overcoming a break-up

As you can see from the above, the clear book ideas typically have a slightly longer description and explain the "What", "Who", "When" and "How" components more strongly – which give the idea its detail. Use these examples to test your book idea against – and work on refining it until it is crystal clear.

Many books were written off a half-baked idea: it wasn't planned out properly before the author wrote it. In rare cases, there have been authors who decided to write a book simply because they wanted to – or because the book idea 'came' to them demanding to be written – and the book did exceptionally well. I have nothing against this, as books that were developed and written in this fashion are often incredible pieces. However, even in this case, I would still invest a portion of time into clarifying the book idea before you unleash your creative spirit onto the page as it will pay dividends later on.

It's important to note here that the clearer your book idea is, the more inspired you will be by it; so, use your internal feeling about your idea as a measuring stick for how clear your idea is. When it's clear, it will 'click'. You will know!

Is It *Unique/Original?*

Since there are literally millions of books in the world, it is important to ensure that your book is unique or original in some way. It is too easy to lightly copy or create a modified version of the most well-known books. Sometimes, we replicate other book ideas without even knowing it! I suggest doing a small amount of research before you begin writing your book – either on Amazon or in book stores – to find out if there is a book like yours already out there. Research like this will also help you to identify which genre your book lives in. If you do find a book that mirrors your idea, don't fret. This is the perfect time to take the essence of your book and rework it with a new angle that differs from the books in your genre.

Find your unique spin on the topic. Formulate your opinion instead of borrowing someone else's. If you are going to teach the 10 steps to "success", then I suggest digging into your own personal life experience to generate your book idea. What is it that you would deeply love to write a book about? Is it success? Or, is it something more specific? Which sub-component of success are you most interested in? You could also view having a unique or original book idea as being specific – and break your general topic, e.g. finances, down into the specific aspect of finances where your knowledge lies. Or, you can find the general theme of your life story, e.g. spiritual awakening, and play strongly on that thread. Ask yourself now, "How unique is my book idea?" and

"How can I make my book idea more unique?" The way to stand out is to be different: and all the world-changing books are.

*Does It **Solve A Problem** or **Answer a Question**?*

It's now time to focus on what problem your book solves or the question it answers. You don't have to provide a cure for cancer in the book to solve a problem. The problem you might solve for the reader could be something as small as healthy meals they can feed their children. Here is a list of just some of the problems your book might solve or questions it might answer for the readers:

- Feeling lost in life – being directionless/purposeless

- Financial struggle or lack

- A need for inspiration and hope

- Gaining greater confidence to meet a partner

- Healing ailments or diseases in the body

- Overcoming trauma or stress

- Thirst for knowledge about an area of life / topic

- Strategies for (x), e.g. building wealth, growing business, write a book

- Poor concentration or memory

- Dis-empowerment in life – all or any area

- Lack of fashion sense

- Insignificance in social status and/or being unpopular

- Bullying or being bullied

- Doubting whether there is a God / divine order

- Wanting to be smarter / more intelligent / have a greater awareness

- High turnover of staff in a company

- Lack of new customers in or to a business

- Connection with the author/another human being, e.g. not feel alone

- To fill empty time, e.g. while on holidays, travelling, commuting

And the list goes on! Take a moment how to write down the need or problem that your book will solve for people:

_____

_____

_____

_____

_____

_____

_____

Being clear on the problem your book helps people with will generate a strong connection between you and the reader(s) and add to your drive and desire to finish the book. Understanding that your book will actually help someone to advance, add to or transform their life in some way turns what would have been some mere words on a page into a powerful and important mission. It has you realize that both what you know and your story are important in this world and that yes, you have a message that matters.

Once you have identified the problem the book solves, you will find it easier to market your book to the world. And, doing this ahead of time will give you a significant advantage by the time you publish, as you are likely to have already developed several creative ideas for how to share the book with people. This will also improve the quality and power in your writing as you will be writing for a strong purpose and towards a specific goal. You will find it easier to write the book for the reader and speak their language.

The following table shows the titles and authors of ten books and the needs they fulfil for the reader. Please note: the needs fulfilled (or problem solved) have been created from my own personal observation only.

#	Book Title	Author	Needs Fulfilled/Problem Solved for the Reader
1	*The Power of Now*	Eckhart Tolle	A quest for presence, stillness, and clarity in life; spirituality.
2	*The Long Walk To Freedom*	Nelson Mandela	Desire for greater understanding of this 'hero's' place in history; possibly inspiring greatness in readers.
3	*The Secret Language of Your Body*	Inna Segal	Solves the problem of illness through awakening our mental power to heal the body.
4	*Jamie's Dinners: The Essential Family Cookbook*	Jamie Oliver	Delivering ideas to parents who struggle to cook for their family and/or children every week.

5	*Dear Lover*	David Deida	Desire to have deeper intimacy and connection (and relationships with) partner(s) – typically designed for women in relation to men.
6	*Think & Grow Rich*	Napoleon Hill	The desire for greater financial wealth through providing mindset and strategic principles to readers.
7	*Business Stripped Bare*	Richard Branson	Educates the reader on the approaches of a billionaire business man; encourages the entrepreneurial spirit.
8	*How to Win Friends & Influence People*	Dale Carnegie	Aspirations for social power and status for people desiring more influence on personal and business levels.
9	*Your Life, Your Legacy*	Roger Hamilton	A greater understanding of ourselves as individuals in relation to establishing financial fortunes and flow; money empowerment and potential.
10	*Eat That Frog*	Brian Tracy	Procrastination!

Use the above examples as inspiration for clarifying the need that your book fulfils. Focus your efforts towards doing exactly that and making a big impact on the lives of your readers. There is another reason behind why your book idea is such an essential stage in book writing, and that can be summarized in a simple formula:

Clarity of book idea = ease of writing

The clearer you are about the details of your book idea, the easier it will be to write. This is partly because a great book idea helps you to organize your thoughts more easily in Step 2 of the book creation process – Structure – and partly because a great book idea will ignite your inspiration. What commonly happens when people don't have a solid book idea is that they get halfway through writing the manuscript, or even a quarter of the way through, and run into a roadblock (fondly known as writer's block). This could be because 1) they got tangled up in their content, 2) because they tried to fit too much content into one book, or 3) they simply ran out of steam (inspiration). And, unfortunately, many people give up and walk away because of this, turning it from an exciting thought into an unfinished project that was pushed to the side.

A great book idea will enable you to write it in any fashion, either in a week or over a year of consistent progress. A great book idea will enable you to revisit the manuscript at any point and still be inspired by it. It will enable you to jump to almost any place within the manuscript and add a paragraph or a page of content, because a great book idea beckons you, stimulates you and inspires you. It engages and calls upon not just the core message of the book, but the core message that you live by. You want the strength of your book idea to outrun the doubts and challenges that will inevitably arise along the journey of producing it. You want your book idea to be so compelling that you yourself can't wait to read it. And, if you weren't the author, you would want to go and buy it off the shelves, simply because the topic is deeply interesting to you and so is the content that you're publishing in it.

Let's Work On Your Book Idea

The following section will help you to overcome the challenge of finalizing your book idea. Some book ideas come easily (like this one, *The Book Within You*), and others require a little bit of love and time. Spend time now filling out answers to the following questions. Give them some thought as you jot down your responses. If you find that your book idea doesn't last the length of the questions – i.e. if you are struggling to find answers, are feeling uninspired, or get seriously stuck – then this might be a sign that the book idea isn't 'the one'.

It can be difficult to simply throw out an idea, but it's wiser to let go and let the higher quality ideas come to you than it is to force the process. If you struggle in the idea stage, you'll struggle in the writing. There is a fine line between persistence and simply being stubborn... believe me, I know! And, it has to be said, that there are more exciting and more inspiring ideas for books to be found. It's worth it to find them, as the worst thing you can do for your writer's spirit is crush it under an uninspiring book idea.

Let's start with a simple question. What book are you writing?

_____

_____

_____

_____

_____

_____

_____

What is the topic of your book? Try to condense it to 1 or 2 topics maximum, as overloading your book with topics will confuse the reader and make it hard to market and sell.

_____

_____

_____

_____

_____

_____

_____

_____

_____

What style of book are you writing?

❑ Memoir

❑ Personal Story with a Message

❑ Interview Style Book

❑ Co-Authored Book

❑ Information Book

❑ How-To Book

❑ Other _____

What genre/topic does your book fit into?

❑ Health & Wellness

❑ Business

❑ Leadership

❑ Finance

❑ Relationships

❑ Self-Help

❑ Spirituality / New-Age

❑ Pregnancy / Maternity

❑ OTHER: _____

There is a large number of genres your book may fit into; however, use the above boxes as a guideline to assist you with gaining clarity.

Does the book touch on local issues? Community? National? Does it have a global message?

_____

_____

_____

_____

_____

What is the message?

_____

_____

_____

_____

_____

_____

What will the reader gain from reading your book?

_____

_____

_____

_____

_____

How will your book change the reader's life? What will it help them achieve?

_____

_____

_____

_____

_____

What is your working title for the book?

_____

_____

_____

What is your working subtitle for the book?

_____

_____

I will go into more detail about titles and subtitles later in the book, so use the lines above for the time being to jot down your current thoughts about what the title and subtitle of your book might be.

When working on your book idea, also keep the following questions in mind:

- **Is This Idea Actually a Book Idea?**

I'm going to start off simply and say that you have to be willing to ask yourself if this idea you feel is a book, is actually a book. Pay attention to whether there is enough content inside you to fill the book, where the content will come from, and how serious you are about turning it into a book. If you conclude it's not a book idea, there is no need for concern: you can also turn your book ideas into blog articles, eBooks and other content. Become fearless about letting go of the many book ideas in order to find the one perfect book idea that truly belongs to you.

- **Is It a Book I Would Love to Write?**

This question reflects back to earlier in the book when I spoke about the book within you being _within_ you: in other words, being a book that you actually care about. Again, if you are not deeply invested nor convinced of the content that the book requires in order to get finished, you will lose interest part-way through and jump ship. And, if you do somehow manage to discipline yourself to finish it, the end result may not be outstanding.

- **Is this Book Idea ONE idea?**

When you sit down to write a book, you can often become excited by finally being able to write your book. And, in this excitement, your book idea can sometimes become tangled as you try to put too much content into one book.

The advantage of teasing out the many ideas within your one book idea is that you end up being a multiple-published author. There is no reason to stop at one book. Your marketing will be ten times easier when you have only one idea inside a book, not two or ten, and you will find it that much easier to talk about and sell the book once it is published.

- **Are My Clients and Marketplace Interested in This Topic?**

Test out whether this is the kind of book that your marketplace wants to read from you. Every leader who is in the public eye has followers. And, the people who follow those them do so because they are interested in the content the person shares, the system they are teaching, the method they present, and so on. They want to know more about it. Where some new authors stumble is that they publish a book that has nothing to do with the ideas their marketplace is interested in reading more about from them. Because the content in the book doesn't match what the marketplace wants to read about, that leader then has to work harder to create or find a following who *are* interested in the content.

Stop for a moment and ask, "Are the people who follow me interested in this topic?" and "Which ideas or content do people follow me for?" In fact, take a moment now to answer exactly this question on the lines below:

_____

_____

_____

_____

Once you have answered the above questions, take your book idea to a select group of people and market-test it to see what responses people give you. Be conscious of who you ask about the book idea. In an ideal world, these won't just be your family, friends or people who tend to encourage you in any pursuit you take on. You want to get an accurate perspective of the book idea, not one biased by adoration! Use these people as a sounding board to test out how clear, unique and original your book idea is as well as gauge the level of interest your followers have in reading a book written by you about that topic.

And now, with a clear, inspiring book idea in hand, it's time to move to Step 2 of the book creation process.

Step 2: Structure

The second step in creating your book manuscript is to initiate a structure for your book. The structure could otherwise be called a "Book Outline" or a Table of Contents. In simplest terms, the structure forms the plan and roadmap for you once you begin writing. It determines what content goes in the book and in what order. Now, I will stress here how important it is to have a structure for your book before you begin writing, because it is a step that a majority of people skim over or skip completely. A book outline has many purposes:

- Brings structure and order to your content

- Provides a skeleton for you to write to

- Makes it easy to slot existing written content into the book manuscript

- Keeps you focused throughout the book writing process

- Enables you to more easily organize your thoughts

- Helps you to 'chunk' the book writing project down into small tasks

- Adds consistency and strength to the book

- Gives you a strong mental grip on the project

- Helps the book to make sense to the reader

- Speeds up the writing process as it guides your focus

- Gives you a bigger picture perspective on your book while writing

- Inspires you to finish the book by being able to see the whole project before you begin writing

- Makes it easier to add ideas to the book later on

- Turns your book into a paint-by-numbers approach

As you can see, there are an incredible number of benefits to creating a book outline. However, let me add to this by giving you a metaphor to communicate how important it is to have some kind of outline for your book. Imagine if you will for a moment the human body without a skeleton. That is like writing a book without a structure: it's a mess! Having a solid, clear book outline will allow you to slot in your 4:00 a.m. bright-ideas more easily, as you will know where they fit in the book or if they fit in the book at all.

Later in the book, I delve deeply into the story of how I wrote my fourth published book, *The Inspirational Messenger: The 5 Pillars to Becoming Inspirational in Everything You Do*, in four days over the 2013 Easter weekend. I will share what I did to create such a beautiful, mystical experience; however, the reason I bring it up now is to make a point about structure. My ability to write a book with such speed was due to, in part, the level to which I planned the book before I began. Difficult as it was, because I was so driven to write the book, I disciplined myself to create the full outline for the book before I even touched the page. My book outline had over 80% of the chapter topics and sub-chapter topics planned out, and I had set a detailed word count target for the book that looked like this:

- 5 Parts (or Pillars, as I called them)
  - 3 Chapters per part
    - 3300 words per chapter
      - Introduction = 500 words
      - 3 x sub-chapters of 900 words each
      - A conclusion of 100 words

Once I had my book structured and I knew how many words were to be written in each section, "all I had to do" was fill them in. I would say to myself, "Write 900 words on how book writing unfurls the brilliance inside us? No problem!" Before I knew it, I had the chapter written. My diligence in planning the book first reaped many dividends and produced one of my most inspiring books.

Now, before we move on to how to actually create a book outline that can organize your thoughts and speed up your writing process, let me show you what the main components of a book typically are. You may modify this structure to suit your book idea (i.e. leaving out an Introduction or not having a Bibliography or even adding another section).

- **Dedication**

   The dedication page of your book sits close to the start of the book, typically before the Table of Contents. It is the author's opportunity to dedicate the book to someone (or many people) special in their life, or someone who contributed greatly to the book being written. An example might be: "Dedicated to my two beautiful sons for the love they bring to my life," or "To my beautiful wife – you are my guiding light."

- **Preface**

   The Preface is an aspect of a book that isn't as commonly used as the others, especially in modern-day books. The purpose of a Preface is to share the story of how the book came to be; an early note from the author (which can also be done in the Introduction). It is also used as an opportunity to thank people who played a role in creating the book (which can also be done in the Acknowledgments).

- **Foreword**

   The Foreword of a book is essentially a long third party endorsement about you (as the author) and the book. Typically 1-2 pages in length (book size, not A4), the Foreword is generally written by someone who is in a similar field, a mentor, and who has equal or greater status than you. The reason for this is that it simultaneously raises the status of your book.

- **Introduction**

  An introduction welcomes the reader to the book, shares a basic synopsis of what is about to come, and tells the reader what they will learn and/or gain from reading the book.

- **Chapter 1 – (x)**

  The chapters of your book are where all the actual content of the book goes. The chapters form approximately 80-85% of the manuscript. They are where you let loose and teach and write to your heart's content. It's important to note here that your chapters may be divided down into 2 or more parts in the book, and in which case, you would typically include a separate sub-title page e.g. "PART 2 – TITLE" in the book in between the chapters. In some cases, authors also include a 1-2 paragraph description to introduce each part in the book.

- **Conclusion**

  The purpose of a conclusion is to wrap up and close off the content or story in the book. In your conclusion, you may choose to remind the reader what they 'got' from the book – e.g. a summary. You can also use this as your opportunity to leave the reader with one final piece of advice, an uplifting message, or your hope for them and their lives.

- **Acknowledgements**

  The Acknowledgments is a part of a book I highly recommend including, as it is your chance to thank the people who contributed to the book, and gratitude is essential in manifesting a great life. The people you thank might range from your editors and publisher to your family and friends.

- **Resources**

  Depending on the nature of your book, you might choose to include a Resources section. The Resources section is an opportunity to suggest additional reading, courses, trainings or information for the reader to help them continue their education on the topic you wrote about.

- **Glossary**

  A Glossary is essentially a list of the main words (usually the more complex terms specific to your field or topic) that you have used throughout the book, accompanied by a definition or explanation of those words. This section assists the reader to gain a deeper understanding of the content in the book by knowing the context and meaning of those terms.

- **Bibliography**

  A bibliography is generally referred to as a list of all the external sources you looked at, studied or reviewed during the process of writing your book: including books, articles, papers, essays, and websites, etc. A bibliography can include the works of other people that you both directly cited and indirectly 'used' to write your book e.g. general background research.

- **References**

  Slightly different from a bibliography, a reference list only details the sources that you directly referred to in your book e.g. quotes, statistics and selected pieces of research. You may choose to utilize a full academic approach to referencing in the 'References' section of your book. I suggest using, at the very least, a bibliography in the back of your book in the case that you are drawing your content and wisdom from someone else's body of work or knowledge.

- **About the Author**

  The About the Author section of your book is a bio about you as the author. In a standard sized book (6 x 9 inch cover), the author bio may take up 250-300 words (approximately a full page) and be positioned beside/around a professional headshot of the author. This bio typically explains the background of the author as well as their accomplishments and what they currently do.

- **"Other Titles By…"**

  Some authors include a page in the back of their book with 'Other Titles by…'. On this page, they show a list of their other books, DVD's, products and so on that they have produced and published and that are for sale. A page of this nature would typically include the cover or a graphic of each product or book, as well as the sale price and a link to where the reader can purchase it from. This particularly applies once you have published more than one book.

- **Sales/Promotion Page**

  Many professional speakers and consultants include what I refer to as a 'sales page' in the back of their book. The sales page is an opportunity for the author to pitch or promote another service or product that they have available in their business. For example, the sales page might invite the reader to attend a free promotional event or a paid event. The prices of the products and services sold via a sales page can be anything from $30 to $5000 and beyond. It all depends on what your business is and what the next step for the reader is.

Make a note to yourself now which components you will be including in your book. It's time to create your book outline. But before we do, let's talk about how many words your book is going to be.

How Long Is A Piece of String?

One of the questions I am asked most frequently about book writing is, "How long should my book be?" or "How many words do I need to write to make a book?" Well, fortunately or unfortunately for you, there isn't a single answer to this question. Every book varies greatly depending on the content in the book and the way in which the book is written and produced – including the size of the cover – and, like people, I've seen all shapes and sizes. How many words your book ends up being depends on your personal aspiration and preference, and of course, how much you feel you have to say on the topic whether it's business or a life story. However, to give you some relief, here are three general guidelines on how long your book might be, based on the core components of a book.

- **To Create Credibility**

  If your goal in becoming an author is to establish a high level of credibility in your field, then I suggest writing a book that has more bulk to it e.g. a book of 60,000 words or more. This will demonstrate to the reader that you have extensive knowledge on that topic – without, of course, creating watered-down content for the sake of making the book thicker.

- **To Get A Message Across Quickly**

  If you would love to produce a book that is a quick-read for people – one that gets your point across in an efficient, effective way – then a book of 35-40,000 words will easily do the job. This will come out as a "handbag book": one that can be read in a few hours or a day.

- **To Share A Personal Journey**

  If you are sharing a personal journey, you might choose to produce a 40,000 word book if you want to share only a part of your story. An autobiography would tend to be more like 80,000 words or more; as it shares the gory details from childhood to adulthood and beyond. This one is more difficult to give guidelines on, as I am lacking information about how you want to present your memoir and how much of your story you want to tell.

Think about your reader when you are choosing how many words the manuscript will be. Are your readers the kind of people that love to devour heavy information? Or, are they busy and so only have time to flick-through a piece? Keep this in mind and research other books in your genre. Use them as a guide. If you are concerned that your book will be too short (or too long), try not to be overly concerned about it as a book can be shortened or lengthened during the production stages. However, I would say that unless you want your book to feel like a booklet (a light handbook, if you will), then I wouldn't tend to write anything under 30,000 words. And, if you don't want to completely overwhelm people, then I would suggest keeping the book under or around 100,000 words.

Decide on Your Book Length

What length is your book going to be (approximately)?

Examples:

❑ 10 Chapters x 3000 words = 30,000 words + Introduction & Conclusion

❑ 20 Chapters x 2500 words = 50,000 words + Introduction & Conclusion

❑ 30 Chapters x 2000 words = 60,000 words + Introduction & Conclusion

_____

What size book are you looking to produce?

_____

The answers to the two questions above may change over time as you write your book: this is fine. This is simply an opportunity to begin getting clear ahead of time, as it will help you to write the manuscript by breaking the project down into smaller bites.

Creating Your Book Outline

The two core stages that happen when creating the outline for your book are 1) listing out all of the content that will be included in the book, and 2) organizing that content into a coherent order and logical structure. Firstly, it involves making a complete list to capture everything that you have ever thought about including in the book from the moment you first conceived or came across the idea.

The following questions will get you thinking about this for your book:

What stories do I want to include in the book?

Which information am I teaching?

Am I sharing a method or process in the book?

Will I be including graphics, images, charts, diagrams, etc.?

Will I be including case studies in the book? Which ones?

Are there any inspiring quotes or words of wisdom I want to share?

Will I be drawing on the knowledge of other people?

Write freely as you create your list of content, in either a Word document or with a good old pen and paper. Don't stop writing until you have captured every thought you have had around what your book is actually about. As you list out your content, you will begin to focus on the order in which that content appears in the book. I do have an uncanny knack for organizing ideas and stories into books – something I do with every one of my private clients – however when the client is detailing what will go in their book, I often notice that a natural order and structure begins to appear. Identify which content is a chapter and what piece is a one-liner. Think laterally and logically about what order the content should appear in. You might choose to follow this five-step approach:

1. Create a list either in a Word Document or on a blank piece of paper

2. Write out all of your ideas for contents and the things you want to write about in the book

3. Circle or highlight the ones that you know are the bigger topics in the book – these will become your chapters

4. Work through and slot all of the other notes – one-by-one – under the chapter headings where they belong

5. Once you have slotted in all the content, sit back and take a break. Then, come back and review it.

It's completely okay to have a small handful of blank spaces in your book outline as you will fill these in as you write the book and content emerges from you. The core purpose of this outline is to make sure that you are going to begin writing a book that has a coherent order to it; and that it presents your content (whether it is story or information) in an appealing way to the reader. Once you have finished your outline, it's important to stick to it closely unless you are willing to recreate it halfway through writing your book. I suggest making only minor changes once you have created your outline to avoid confusion later on.

Work on your book outline with patience. Give it the attention it needs and don't sign off on it until you are clear and satisfied with the order and emerging theme of content in your book.

The Book with No Gaps

The final point I want to make when it comes to structuring your book is about writing a book that has no 'gaps'. Writing a book with no gaps is about making sure that when you move from Chapter 1 to Chapter 2, that you have properly finished explaining the content in Chapter 1 (doing it justice) and then leading the reader into the content coming up in Chapter 2. See, some writers will dump all their content into individual documents and then just slap them together into one word document, forming what they now call a book. The unfortunate side-effect of this is that the reader is then left, often, to make up their own mind about how the ten topics fit together, if at all, instead of being neatly led from chapter to chapter, with each chapter placed where it is with purpose and intention. On the flipside of this, there are other writers who understand how important it is that all their content is in its right place and connected together beautifully. When you read their books, you get the sensation of it being hard to put the book down.

To understand this further, let me explain a model that I use when I am coaching clients called *The Book Pyramid*. *The Book Pyramid* looks like this:

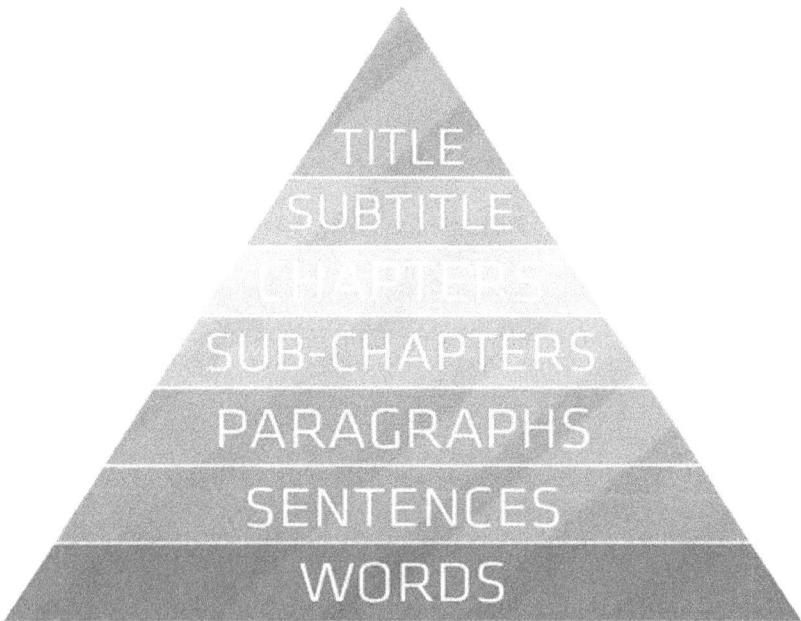

This graphic has been created to show how all of your ideas can be connected to a bigger idea: ultimately the core idea of the book, and therefore the main message. The title will ideally represent and be the pinpoint for the core message of your book. It has the greatest impact and captures the essence of the book. Below that, the subtitle supports the title and gives further explanation to what the book is about. Then, the chapters come in below that, each one supporting and fitting under the title and subtitle. Every piece of content in every one of your chapters has the purpose of further explaining the message that is in the title and subtitle. Then, within each chapter, the sub-chapters support the main message of that single chapter. Then, within sub-chapters, you then have the paragraphs, which serve the purpose of explaining the topic of the sub-chapter. And of course, last but not least you have sentences and then words.

The idea of this graphic is to provide you with a visual guide that will assist you to stay on purpose and to eliminate unnecessary tangents within your book. It will assist you to write a book where all the content and stories are connected together and flowing nicely. Imagine it to be like a massage. Some of the greatest massages I've had are the ones where the massage therapist doesn't take your hands off you, not even to walk around the table to work on your other side. They will keep a few fingers on you as they circle the table, which creates the experience of being cared for. This is what you want to create for your readers; you want them to not ever feel alone, not even for one moment or syllable of your book. The more well-structured your content is, and the more tightly you weave it together, the more you will create this feeling for them. Don't leave them wondering – explain it. Don't leave a detail out – define it. Don't skip details – share them. Stay present with the reader throughout the text; take them on a journey through the pages of your book.

It's worth it to spend enough time clarifying your book outline, regardless of how complex or simple the structure of your book may be. Even if you only plan the book to 60%, it will give you a winning advantage over the many other writers who make no plan at all, which as we know, can be a form of planning to fail. Trust yourself. You can do this.

Step 3: Write

The next step in the book creation process it to write the content. Step 3, writing, is the most time intensive part of becoming an author. It is literally about getting the words out and down onto the page, fleshing out all of your ideas, sharing your stories and bringing your content together to form a book. There are several approaches to achieving this and completing this stage of book creation. Let's run through these now so that you can choose which one(s) you will be utilizing in order to write your book.

Write It Yourself

This approach is perhaps the most common, and naturally it involves you being willing, eager and prepared to sit down to type the content for your chapters. I would have to say from personal experience that this is often the most rewarding way to bring a book to life; however, it also requires the greatest mastery. Writing your book by typing it will empower you to stand on bigger stages and take your message to the world. I will provide you with tips and insights throughout the remaining chapters of this book as I endeavour to be the best guide I can be for your journey.

Speak Your Book

The second approach that I've seen many people utilize in book writing is to 'speak' their book. Now, in some cases, people will literally sit with a Dictaphone in hand and simply talk about their content into the device. Then, they have the audio files transcribed and, typically, employ a book writer or editor to blend the content together to make a book. In other cases, they will take the keynote presentations or courses that they do, audio record them, and again, use the transcripts to formulate the many pages of their book. And, in the third and final case, 'speaking your book' may involve setting up a series of interviews with a team member or third party about your content and audio recording each one.

Many high profile individuals – some that you may know well – use these approaches to create their book, as it has the ability to save time and make the book creation process more efficient. There are several things to keep in mind when choosing to create your book in this way, the most important of which is to have a clear outline. When we speak, we have a greater tendency to go off on tangents, and this can create a lot of unnecessary hard work to clean up the transcripts and turn them into a manuscript.

Interview People

The third approach you can take to generate the content for your book is to interview people. Now, it's important to note here, that this approach would typically be used if your book is an interview-style book (like my book, *Transformational Leaders*) and you are featuring the lives of several people or experts or if you are utilizing case studies or stories from people to back up and emphasize the message you are writing. This isn't intended as an easy-way-out of writing (e.g. don't use interviews with people because you can't be bothered thinking up great content), but merely as a guide in case you are actually planning on creating a book using content or stories from other people as a core feature.

In hindsight, *Transformational Leaders* was one of the easiest books I've put together. It took me less than two weeks to produce the manuscript in total if I had condensed the time down into a single time block. I interviewed 13 people for an hour to an hour and a half each, had the audios transcribed and edited each one up (which took me about 1-2 hours per interview) into a chapter. With a few edits, it was complete. This isn't to say that the book didn't require the same persistence as all my others have, because it certainly did at times, but the process of getting the words on paper was relatively straightforward.

Researching Content

The fourth way you can write your book is through presenting research. This will undoubtedly involve long hours of reading, live interviews and Googling in order to draw a conclusion about your topic before you can present that into a book. You may organize the chapters of your book into the ten main discoveries you made while researching, or the ten main points within the one large discovery. A book that involves a high level of researching might also involves a high level of referencing; something that I urge you to do carefully. If you attended University, now is the time to bring those referencing skills back and let them work for you!

Hire a Ghost-writer

The final way that you can get your content down on paper is to hire a ghost-writer. There are advantages and disadvantages to working with ghost-writers. The upside of a ghost-writer is that it tends to save you time as you are not the one doing all of the typing. An experienced ghost-writer will tend to interview you personally to create the content, making the process smoother and less time-consuming for you. Leading speakers and business owners tend to utilize ghost-writers as a means of producing the book more quickly than if they had produced it themselves. Other people flat out dislike writing, and a ghost-writer saves them from hours of frustration. And, in some cases, ghost-writers actually produce a higher quality book than the author would have.

There are however, a few downsides that it's wise to be aware of before you work with a ghost-writer. First of all, they can certainly come with a price tag of $10,000 and above: a price which is often justified by the extreme dedication and hard work that it takes to produce someone else's book. It is also quite easy to become emotionally-mentally disconnected from the content and the book itself when someone else is producing the manuscript. It then becomes easier to skip over important to detail or wind up with a book that didn't capture your message or story the way you wanted.

And the final downside, I believe, has to do with conscience. A ghost-writer can quite easily add their own intellectual property, opinions, and ideas to a manuscript when writing: sometimes it's unavoidable (I know because I've done it). The book then becomes a combination of content from the author and ghost-writer, which in my view rubs up against the principle of producing a book: to share your content and ideas. You want your readers to feel that what they are reading came from you and that you care about it. If you can efficiently manage these downsides of using a ghost-writer and are willing to invest in the book to have it produced, then I have no issue recommending it as an approach to achieving your goal.

My final input on choosing ghost-writing as the method for creating your book is to make sure that you're not doing it to dodge the writing process, because, for example, you think you're not a good writer but, in your heart, you would love to write. As I have no doubt said already, writing is an extremely rewarding process, and one not to be missed out on. So, choose wisely!

Regardless of the approach you choose to utilize in Step 3: Write, I suggest being present through this stage of book creation. Your end product will end up being higher quality and the response you get from your readers will reflect this. And, beyond that, you will be so much more satisfied with the end product, which is a priceless feeling to have. As you write your book, focus on the meaning. Focus on getting the messages across and let the words shape themselves around that. And that, sums up the third stage in the book creation process – Write.

Step 4: Review

In the review stage, you will be reviewing your own content and improving it with a final work-over. It is a part of the process during which you need to become semi-objective related to your book. Now, be aware: the review of your book is a very different stage compared to the writing stage, and in my explaining it, you will see how and why. The review stage has the following core purposes:

- **Confirming that all the content is present**

   The first purpose of a book review is to ensure all the content that you intended to include in the book, is actually in the book. This is your chance to check you haven't missed anything or left anything out.

This might include making sure that you have told all parts of a story, included all diagrams, and finished all your sentences.

- **Quality-control**

  Naturally, the review stage of book writing is a great opportunity – and the main one, I might add – to check over how 'good' the book is. During review, you will be checking whether all the content makes sense, if the book is well-written, and if you find it entertaining and interesting. It's your chance to ask yourself whether you are satisfied with what you have written. Does the book flow nicely? Is the content in the right, logical order? Is it all linked together? Is it easy to read?

- **Personal satisfaction**

  Personal satisfaction is closely related to quality control, although this one is more personal. Reviewing your book thoroughly provides you with the opportunity to see if you personally are in love with your own book. Are you satisfied with your efforts? Have you done your message and original intention justice? Did you get to say what you wanted to say? Do your stories and information accurately reflect what was in your mind? Does the book inspire you?

One of the problems that some people have when they're writing their book is that they start to criticize, critique and review it before they have finished writing it. They begin to judge their writing content, wonder if it's any good, and try to polish the manuscript before the initial content is even complete. I smack my clients on the hand whenever they try to do this! Here's why.

The writing process is highly creative: your main focus is to create content. It is about output. It's about building something. It's about filling the pages with amazing content and bringing the vision of your book to life. In direct contrast with this, the review stage, is a more grounded stage where we begin to encounter elements like getting other people's feedback and suggestions, reading it ourselves from an external perspective, and then looking at what improvements can be made. The review stage should only occur when at least 95% of your writing is complete. Reviewing only happens once you have laid the foundation.

Some people can become highly sensitive during the review stage of their manuscript. It's like having your sixth grade English teacher put red marks all over your work! However, despite it being challenging at times, the review stage is crucial as it takes your book from good to great. I used to be uncomfortable having people reviewing my content, and I even struggled to do it myself. One of my earlier tricks was to use a different coloured pen besides red so that the process wouldn't feel so much like English class in high school. Then, as I got more and more comfortable coming face-to-face with my own content, I returned to the red pen which I now love, since I appreciate the review stage of all of my books. Here is how I recommend that you perform a review of your book:

1. Print and Bind the Manuscript

   The first step is to print and bind your manuscript. This can be nerve-racking to do because reading a manuscript printed out is a different ball game to reading it on a computer screen. God knows why, but the words simply look and feel different on paper. You will immediately notice the weak spots and mistakes in the book... which is exactly why I want you to print it out!

2. Read Through The Book One Page At A Time With A Pen... and Write All Over It!

   Work through the book patiently and make notes on your own content. Circle parts that don't work. Add others notes if you missed something. Give it your energy, love and devotion. Focus on filling in gaps, identifying errors, and making sure your messages flow. You will come across areas where you went off on a tangent. When you do, decide whether to take the content out (be it 1-5 paragraphs or two whole pages) or weave it in so it fits more tightly into the book. You might also come across chapters that are weaker than others; and decide to re-do them. Anything and everything is permitted in the review stage: this is about recreating, refining and improving.

The most powerful thing about the review stage of book creation is that it allows you to have the hands-on experience of turning something ordinary into something extraordinary. Now, your book may have already been extraordinary before you began reviewing but as one of my high school English teachers said to me, "You can edit an A-grade piece of work over and over and still find ways to change or improve it." In other words, there is always another level that you can go to with the book.

Side note here: if you read your book and you get bored then we have a problem because it's your content! And, if you don't love it, the likelihood of others loving it, is lower. To make it more interesting you might add more stories. Or, you might add a bit of humour. It might be a bit too dark or heavy to read, so then you uplift it or take a little bit out and add a bit. That's what the review stage is all about. It is markedly about improvement. By the time you're done with the review stage you should be able to say "Yes I'm absolutely satisfied with my content. I love it. I'm finished." This is the feeling to aim for before your book goes to the next stage of production.

Getting External Feedback

I want to address an essential topic here; getting feedback from other people on your book during the review stage. Now, many people love to hand the book to a few people to get their thoughts on it; i.e. "Do you like it?" so that they can improve upon it before it goes to print. I agree that it can be a valuable experience to receive people's feedback on your book. However, there are two things I want you to keep in mind when you do so:

- **Is this person my target reader?**

  The first is to consider whether the person you are handing your manuscript to is your target reader. You want to be conscious of who you hand your book to as placing it in the hands of someone who isn't interested in the least in your content can result in you receiving a series of harsh, and quite frankly, inaccurate feedback on your book. So, choose people who are not just friends and family, but also clients who don't know you as well and who are distant enough to give you honest feedback. My general advice? If they wouldn't buy or read a book on that topic, don't ask for their view on it.

Bear in mind that the person reviewing will tend to give you advice to change the book to how *they* want it, as opposed to how it would best serve the readers. And, if the person you are handing the book to is much more distant than a close contact, you might consider having them sign a non-disclosure agreement before hitting send on the email: just in case.

- **Is this person too close to me?**

It's a beautiful thing that our friends and family usually tend to support and encourage us on going for our dreams (generally speaking). However, this can be a downside when it comes to getting feedback on your book. Be careful that you aren't handing your book to someone who will say, "Yes, dear, it's lovely," for the sake of pleasing you because they care about you. You will grow maximally when you source feedback from people who will help you to craft it into a higher quality manuscript and give you ample suggestions for how you can improve the book.

Once the review stage of your book is complete, it is time to move to the fifth and final stage of manuscript creation: editing.

Step 5: Edit

The fifth and final stage of creating the manuscript for your book is the editing stage. Editing is crucial and completely different from all of the four stages that have come before it. The first thing I will say on editing is that it is essential that you don't edit your own book. Despite my experience in professional editing, I don't edit my own books. I understand how important it is to have the book looked over thoroughly from top-to-toe by a professional. If I edit the manuscript myself, I *know* that I will miss errors and that there will be improvements that could be made that will go unnoticed by me: purely because I am too close the project. And so are you, so please, delegate it!

The editor is a person who looks over the manuscript, working through it line-by-line and paying attention to components like grammar, punctuation, fact-checking and so on. If they are an experienced editor, they will give you feedback on how to improve the book, although in many cases, editors simply work with what you have given them. It's essential the editor you choose has a) plenty of experience in editing, and b) the language you write in as their first language (or are fluent in your language). You want the editor to be in their natural tongue when checking over your manuscript as both punctuation and grammar change drastically between languages. This will enhance the quality of their work as they go through your book chapter-by-chapter. At the end of the editing process, you will be reading your book as it will be read by the editors (minus the final stages of production and publish including proof reading). This is their main role: to make your book reader-ready.

What If I Don't Like My Edited Book?

It's possible that you may not like the edited version of your manuscript. I worked as an editor for a client many years ago who had this exact experience. When he read the edited version of the book, he was surprised at how different parts of the book sounded after going through professional editing, to the point where he felt put-off by the whole process. However, after sending the unedited and edited manuscript to a few close contacts, he quickly realized that the book actually did sound better than the original. In other words, it was more professional, cleaner and polished: which is the primary goal of an editor. So, it's important that you are tolerant through the editing process. Keep your primary goal in mind – to improve your manuscript – and be willing to work with your editor to achieve this outcome.

Editing will typically change the 'voice' the book is written in slightly. This is completely normal, all of my books encounter it, and it is nothing to be taken personally. Another thing to bear in mind is that it's not wise to expect your editor to either like or dislike your content. Their job is to improve what is; the content that is already on the paper. In many cases, the editor will actually tell you what they think of the actual content, however they may reserve their opinion for the sake of remaining objective and performing a more thorough job. So, it's wise not to push them for their view on it: leave that to your readers! This brings us to the completion of the *5 Step Process of Book Creation*.

I have some good news for you... you've just finished reading the chapter of the book that is the most content-intense with the highest word count! It's all downhill from here, baby! From *Chapter 6* onwards, you will begin working with your book outline to turn it into a book by filling in the sections and creating the first draft of your manuscript. I will be guiding you through some other practical components that you must keep in mind while you are writing, show you how to overcome obstacles like writer's block, coach you on the authors mindset, and invite you to a greater experience of book-writing... the one that I am so-familiar with. You will have the chance to reflect on your own life in greater depth as you continue to write and become ever-more clued in on how to produce a book that flies.

Chapter 5: What's Your Author Style?

"A word is not the same with one writer as with another. One tears it from his guts. The other pulls it out of his overcoat pocket."

Charles Peguy

*I*n this chapter, I will share the five primary ways people tend to write books: let's call them 'author styles'. In understanding the different approaches people take to writing their book, you can identify which approach suits you best. It may help you to work out why you have struggled to write in the past: because you may have tried to write in a way that simply doesn't work for you. It's only when you are working against your flow that you experience what most people call 'writer's block', where you butt your head against the computer screen, stare at the blank page, or rip up pieces of paper in frustration. If you understand your writing flow, you can understand how you function best as a writer... and then you can write!

It's likely that you will cross over between author styles depending on the stage of your life you are in and the type of book you are producing. This is normal. In fact, I even recommend that, once you have identified your primary author style, that you try one or more of the others to gain more experience. I have personally written (out of curiosity and sometimes necessity) in all of the following five styles, and they all have value to offer. However, I do believe that each person has one dominant style that, put simply, fits them the best. Let's explore them now, starting with The Methodical Writer.

#1 – The Methodical Writer

The Methodical Writer is someone who enjoys the process of gradually writing their book. They like to piece it together with a slow and steady approach: one paragraph, one page and one chapter at a time. They are deeply patient with the process of bringing a book come to life as they work away on their manuscript diligently. They love the process of writing and feel that the experience of producing the book is as delicious as holding it in your hands once it has been published. Because of this, The Methodical Writer can take several months or even years to finish their masterpiece. More often than not, they will choose to invest a longer period of time into perfecting their first draft. They are rarely concerned about how quickly a book is produced; something that I can only vaguely relate to as I tend to feel a sense of urgency when I write books. This author style will feel satisfied whether they write 100 or 10,000 lines in a sitting and are content to chip away at their manuscript until the moment where it can be considered finished.

The Methodical Writer tends to be thorough in their writing style, choosing words carefully, and is particular about how they place their words on the page. Each statement they type will be done so with intent and precision. They are unafraid of paying attention to the finer details of their text, which may drive other people crazy, but many editors will love. They can also be quite spiritually tuned-in, in the sense that they enjoy the personal transformation, mental expansion, the challenge, and the learning curve that often occurs as they write their manuscript. They aren't necessarily impatient to finish the book and believe that if you're going to write a book, then you may as well do it justice and produce a literary masterpiece.

#2 – The Channeller

The Channeller is the type of writer who enters a heightened state of mind when their pen touches the page. They 'download' information, insights, inspiring messages, and wisdom from a higher source – often referred to as the infinite intelligence, soul, collective consciousness, or greater power – and bring it through their mind and hands onto the page. They often feel as though what they write isn't really their own and that it came from "somewhere else."

The Channeller usually writes books in a shorter time span than a Methodical Writer. They cannot predict exactly when the channelling will occur, but when it does, hours can pass by and thousands of words can appear in front of them. If you are a Channeller, you will understand what I mean when I say that time and space will appear to vanish when you write. You may feel as though you have entered a parallel state of mind. It could be debated where exactly The Channeller is 'channelling' from. Some might say the soul, some might say from the heart or mind, and others might say the source of all human life. But, regardless of where the messages are coming from, it has to be said that the writing of a channeller will often have a mystical, magical feeling about it right from the moment it was created. Upon reading it, people will tend to feel uplifted and inspired, and their lives are transformed in the act of reading it. Writings from The Channeller could also be regarded as inspirational teachings or divine messages.

#3 – The Researcher

The Researcher is an author style that I admire. They are the kind of author who loves to devour all the information possible about their topic before they begin the process of compiling the wisdom into a published work. There is an inherent desire within them to know as much as possible and to broaden their knowledge base before they begin teaching others. In fact, books written by The Researcher can be books that present all of their research, not necessarily books that argue or go into great depth on their own personal opinions.

The Researchers are the ones who often have 10, 20, 30 or more years of experience in their field and quite frankly, they are simply brilliant. Geniuses, even. Their books tend to be more like a PhD: at least, in terms of the intelligence they have packed into the pages! In most cases, their books would blow you away. In some cases, The Researcher will perform all of the background reading and accumulation of notes so that, when they do sit to write, they are one hundred percent certain that their book is the best out there on that topic and that the information is sound. Rather than writing about what 'could-be', they may want to write about 'what is' and then lead in to what 'could-be' or how that information can assist people.

Books written by people who are dominant in this author style are usually highly educational with well-presented content, a method or formula to teach. It's not uncommon to find graphs, charts, and other images of a similar nature inside books authored by researchers. They love to learn. When they present their content to readers, they want to make sure the reader has a deep understanding of the topic of their book by the time they close the cover. The Researcher is often an effective teacher and has a high value on knowledge and information. For them, to know is to be great. To share what you know is to be even greater.

#4 – The Brewer

Welcome to author style number four: The Brewer. I often encounter clients who are "Brewers". I love and am equally as fascinated by them. The Brewers are people who have been thinking about their book or the content in their book for a long, long, long time before they begin writing a book. They often have life stories filled with adversities that have proven to be inspirational to the people around them. They have often been told on several occasions by the people around them, "You should write a book."

The Brewer is, in general, a deep thinker and feeler. They reflect on life deeply and when they write, they prefer to write something they personally, strongly believe in (rather than pour their heart out in a book right up front). They will often publish an extraordinary and meaningful book when they eventually do publish a work. I have observed that The Brewer often has high standards on themselves and with this, comes their inherent desire for their book to have a deep and lasting impact on the reader. Their writing may happen quickly or slowly, depending on how urgent they feel it is to get their profound insights or life story out into the world. They don't have a need to back everything they write up with facts or statistics the same way that a Researcher might as their life and professional experience speaks volumes on its own.

#5 – The Enthusiastic Writer

The final of the five primary author styles is The Enthusiastic Writer. The Enthusiastic Writer is like an excited puppy dog when it comes to writing a book. Simply put, they are excited about the possibilities that lay ahead of them by putting thoughts, ideas and feelings onto paper. They are often an extremely social people-person. They love to connect with their readers. For them, writing a book is a playground: another way to communicate with whomever else is 'out there' and willing to listen. They will often want to write a book just to confirm they're not alone in the universe or the journey of life.

The Enthusiastic Writer usually wants to write their book overnight and will put aside time every day if they have to.... because becoming a published author is just so exciting! This treasured author style is often someone who has wanted to write a book but simply hasn't believed that it was possible up until now, or they require someone to believe in them deeply before they could unleash their energy onto the page. Once they know that it's possible, watch out! Their infectious energy will bring what is no-doubt an amazing book to the hands of their readers.

Take a moment now to identify which author style reflects. Which one matches your preferred writing style closest?

_____

Now, for your further reference, identify your second and third primary styles:

2nd: _____

3rd: _____

Regardless of which author style you relate to, it's important that you don't compare yourself to people who write in a different style to you or, even the people who write in the same primary flow as you do. Everyone is different, and your creative process is just as important, valuable and powerful as anyone else's. So, be sure to honour your own writing style and journey equally. While I prefer to write my books in shorter time frames (I am predominantly The

Channeller and The Enthusiastic Writer), I have clients who are very content to have steady progress on their book over the course of a year.

One particular client comes to mind when I think of this: she worked away diligently on her book for about ten months straight. Even if she worked for 15 minutes a day, she was satisfied with her efforts… and her book is magnificent! So, become more intimately familiar with your style over time. Which writing flow feels the most natural to you? Where do you feel the most at home when writing? Let go of comparisons to other people, as that is only going to slow you down when you are writing. Honour your uniqueness. Learn about it. Study yourself. Figure out what works for you and use it to your advantage.

Chapter 6: Getting into the Writing Zone

"And the day came when the risk to remain tight in a bud was more painful than the risk it took to bloom."

Anais Nin

You have crossed a great terrain by the time you reach this chapter. You have become present with the essential foundation for becoming a published author: why you dream of writing this book. You have identified the finer details of the book that is about to come to fruition (because of you, I might add: it's important to realize just how valuable you are as the author). You have explored your vision for the book and given thought to where the ripple effect of your book could go. And now, if every one of these has been successfully ticked off, you are ready to begin writing – and I hope by this stage, you are itching to do just that.

This chapter will help you to open the floodgates. It's about letting the book that has been living within you for days, weeks, months or years, out! I refer to the experience of starting the book as "opening the floodgates" purely for the reason that many of the clients I work with feel that their book was yearning to make its way out of their heart and mind onto the page. They could feel the words building up, ready to overflow as a waterfall of words. There is a powerful release that occurs when you begin writing: when you finally put pen to paper. It can be a vulnerable experience and yet it is incredibly liberating. It is where you begin expressing what is within you and simultaneously crafting a new future for yourself by charging boldly forth towards your goal of becoming an author. It is about crafting new futures for the readers and showing them what is possible for them in their life. It is a deeply rewarding experience, to say the least. In order to have your experience of getting into the writing zone, let's explore how you can create the ideal writing situation for yourself.

The Perfect Writing Situation

I have been asked numerous times what the 'perfect' writing condition is; in other words, what is the secret code that I use in order to get deeply in flow where the words pour out of me. The perfect writing situation includes your internal and external world. It is certainly about the physical environment you place yourself in to write – and the many elements of that environment which I'm about to explore with you – but it is equally if not more about your internal environment. This relates to the state of mind you are in when you sit down to write your book. Setting up your internal environment can be more difficult than setting up any physical space, which is why we're going to talk about physical environments first. Walk with me as we work step-by-step to create your ideal writing environment.

Your Book Is A Product of Your Environment

Your physical environment is made up of many aspects. The first of these is related to your physical body: your home on Earth. The better quality the support you provide yourself physically, the more present and able you will be to write. The following is a simple checklist to follow to help you take care of your body while you write. These are simple – the basics – but they are important. They can interfere with your creative process if left unattended to. I laugh at that, because it makes it sound like writing is an extreme sport, but in all seriousness, it's important to remember that taking care of your body can make the difference between a productive day and one where you sit staring at the screen.

MY BODY

- Am I warm enough?

- Am I cool enough?

- Am I sitting comfortably?

- Am I breathing deeply?

- Am I exhausted?

- Am I hungry?

- Am I thirsty?

- Is the chair I'm on supportive enough?

- Am I sick or well?

- Are my clothes comfortable to write in?

WHERE I WRITE

The next component to examine when setting up the perfect physical environment to write in relates to your physical location. Paying attention to this has the power to provide the inspiration you need to become a powerhouse with words.

First of all, let's talk about where you are on a smaller scale. What I mean by this is what room of the house you are in. Are you in the room that is most conducive to writing? Can you work there for hours undisturbed? You will find that your own home will have rooms and places within those rooms that aid or hinder the creative flow. Take a moment to walk through your house or apartment and take note of which ones these are. It might be your office, your sunroom, your bedroom, your den, your lounge room, or hey, even your kitchen. See and feel which ones feel better for writing the book.

Next, consider that your own home space may not be your preferred writing environment. You might be the kind of person who likes to take their laptop to a café or library and produce your masterpiece there and not just for the sake of looking cool at Starbucks, but because being around other people that you don't know assists your creative process. I personally feel quite connected to my readers when there are people all around me, like in a hotel lobby, airport or café. And so, being in public often assists the writing process. What works best for you?

THE ROOM I'M IN

It's time to pay attention to what room you are specifically sitting in. Is it too crowded? Is it too light? Is it too dark? Are there too many or not enough people around you? You might explore every room of your home until you find the sweet spot... and then get into your groove when you are there. Make it your zone for book production. Set up a sacred space for your writing journey.

OTHER ELEMENTS

There are other elements to consider when setting up the perfect physical writing environment. Forgive me if I have missed some, as there will certainly be different ones for different writers. Naturally, we are all different in personality and preferences, and therefore what aids us to get in the zone will vary greatly from person to person.

- **Music**

    Many people, like myself, adore the experience of writing to music. I have been known to write to house or progressive trance music while producing manuscripts. Do you write to music? If so, which music? The tunes you choose can be influential in how the words land on the page and how much you enjoy the experience of writing. I've known authors to write novels to dramatic music and others to write to peace out to classical and relax while producing their book. You can either choose a music that inspires you (my personal suggestion) or you can actively choose a style of music that will help you to write that particular stage of your manuscript e.g. choose rock music when you want to get a message across powerfully, or romantic music when tuning in to the depth of feeling in a story.

- **Silence**

I quickly learned in my live writing trainings that many people simply prefer the sweet sound of silence when writing. If this is you, bear in mind that you will need to set up your environment to be conducive with this. Write when the kids are at school, when everyone is asleep at night, on your days off, or while tucked away in a log cabin in the Rocky Mountains. Do whatever it takes to get the silence you need: it might just be the key to your golden words.

- **Social Interaction**

It sounds crazy to think that you can be social *and* write at the same time... but it's true! As a writer, I thrive off the connection I have with the people around me; the people who are going to be reading the book. And so, I make a conscious effort to stay connected to people while I am writing, as I know it greatly assists my creative process. Sometimes this is as simple as taking a few hours out at a café to write a chapter. Or, posting on social media platforms and sharing the journey. Other times, I will (shock-horror) chat to friends or clients online during weekend writing sessions, updating them on my progress and sharing parts of the book. Observe now whether you require social interaction around you while writing – the comforting, energy of people –to spur you on.

- **Time of Day**

    The time of day you write may also have an influence on how deeply you get into the zone when working on your book. Some people are naturally night owls and so they can commonly be found producing their content until the wee hours of the morning: long after everyone else has gone to bed. I personally relate to this. There are few things I adore more than a good late night writing session, often while listening to great music. Other people are morning people and so prefer to work on their manuscripts as soon as they wake up in the morning. Identify which time of day is the optimal for you to focus on your writing. Then, schedule it into your calendar.

Now that we have addressed the physical elements that contribute to you opening your floodgates and writing your book, it's time to move to something much more personal: you.

Your Book Is A Product of You

Feeling ready to begin writing can be a hundred times more challenging than setting up your physical environment to induce writing flow. It requires you to take your attention off the world around you and draw your attention to what is within you: your feelings and thoughts. The book you write is a product of you and, therefore, your state of mind while writing will determine what kind of book you write. To assist you in every way I can to enter 'the zone', I have detailed the core issues I personally address when I know I have writing to do. You might call this my internal checklist: the three simple main aspects I look to if I am struggling to write during my allocated time. You can use these to become unstuck and tap into your flow.

1. Becoming Present

    It's difficult to pour out thousands of words (or even a few hundred) when your attention is anywhere but on your book. Notice where your focus is as you sit down to write: are you being distracted by a problem in your life? Are you mentally prepared and ready to write? Are you present with the content you want to add to your book? Or in other words, are you present with your book? The more present you are with it, the more you will enjoy it and the easier it will be to write. A present mind is a powerful mind. Writing while present will create a far more interesting and engaging book for people to read.

2. Dealing with Stress and Challenges

One of the biggest sources of distraction from writing is unresolved stress and challenge. If you just left your partner or you are going through a loss of job (significant life events). it may be more difficult to devote your energy to the book. Despite the rare case where you become driven by the pain of the adversity and pour it into the book (struggle can be a powerful source for writing), I suggest dealing with the more pressing issue at hand. For example, if something was falling apart in my business – let's say a website crashed – I would find it hard to focus on my writing until that was resolved. So, use your intuition: if there is an urgent problem that needs your urgent attention – even if that means taking 24 hours away from the book to care for yourself – attend to it. Then, come back to the book when you're ready.

3. Identifying How You Feel

I believe how we feel when we sit down to write influences what we write and, therefore, how it sounds and feels to the reader. I believe that it's wise to work with, not against your feelings as you write. If you are feeling unwell or exhausted physically, it might not be the ideal time to write. Or, it might be the best time to write, because you're tucked up in bed with a cold and no one to disturb you (finally). If you feel like your life is falling to pieces – break-ups, fights, change in direction – it might not be the best time to write... or it might be the best time, as you will be more enrolled in the message you are sharing. Use your inner wisdom to decipher your feelings and choose how to use them on the path to write your book.

Pay attention to your state of mind before and as you sit down to write. Monitor it as you go. Notice if you're writing something that actually, you don't even agree with (yes, it happens). Observe the difference in your writing when you feel grateful to when you are, simply put, pissed off. Notice how you feel when you write about what you are interested in versus what you're not. Start to master what makes you tick from the inside; what it is that stimulates your creativity and fires you up from within to write. Become a master of your mind. You are your best team member when it comes to writing your book.

Writing A Powerful Introduction

Now that you are ready to write, it's time to begin. Many of my clients and participants from trainings have asked me where the best place to start writing is once you have an idea, vision and outline for your book. While I don't believe that there is a place in your book that you must start, I do believe that there is one place to start that can help you to, well, start: the introduction. The introduction to your book is just that: an introduction. An effective introduction will typically do the following two things: one, emotionally and mentally engage the reader, and two, leave the reader feeling intrigued enough to read the rest of the book. Writing the introduction is a great way to warm up to writing your book: you might think of it like stretching your limbs before you go for a run. The introduction for your book also serves the purpose of warming your reader up for what is about to come in the chapters ahead. It has a few main purposes:

- Telling the reader what the book is about

- Revealing what the reader will get out of the book

- Showing the reader that you understand them and the problems they face

- Showing the reader what you know or believe is possible for them Introducing yourself more personally through story

- Drawing the reader in – getting them engaged

Here are some pointers for writing a strong introduction:

- Be very clear on your intention for the book

- Clearly communicate what the book is about

- Share a 'hook' – story, example, etc. – that draws the reader in

- Have a strong opening line

Sit and get present.... think about your entire book... see the end product in your mind... and then open your eyes and write your introduction. The most important element of all those mentioned in the list above is arguably the first one: to emotionally and mentally engage the reader. Now you may be familiar with the notion of a 'hook'. This term is most commonly used in sales and marketing where experts tell business owners their marketing must have a 'hook'; in other words, something that catches the attention and interest of the prospect and lures them in for a sale. Well, the same applies for your book and readers. Every word you put on the page is essentially there to 'sell' the reader into buying one or many copies of your book... no pressure!

Like we covered earlier, different people buy books based on different components, and flicking to the Introduction is certainly one of those. Hence, it is even more important to make sure that you open your book in an engaging and captivating way. And even more important still, once the reader has purchased the book, how interesting your introduction is will keep them reading into Chapter 1, 2, 3 and hopefully, until the very last page of the book. In an ideal world, you would 'hook' the reader and keep them coming back for all of the books that you write in your lifetime. As you are crafting your hook, you will then begin to think about the rest of your introduction. Think about the following questions when you are writing your introduction:

- Why did I write this book?

- What inspired me to write this book?

- Who has this book been written for?

- What topics are being covered in the book?

- What value is the reader going to get from the book?

- What is the reader going to learn?

- How is the reader going to feel?

- What is going to change in the readers' life because of the book?

- What will this book guide the reader to do or achieve?

- What does the reader need to know before they begin the book?

Crafting your introduction as the first step in your book writing journey will assist you to become present with the book you are about to write. It not only welcomes the reader to the book, but also you as the author. If you are struggling to write your introduction, it usually indicates that you don't have enough clarity in your book idea and outline. Once you are crystal clear on the book, you will be itching to write the introduction. In fact, the words will form in your mind before you touch fingers to keyboard. You might even know what the opening line or story for your book is going to be long before you make the time to sit and write. So, if the introduction feels like a difficult task, I suggest you stop for a moment and review your book idea. Revisit your outline, revisit your content and finally, revisit your vision for yourself and the book. Are you writing a book that inspires you? Can you see how becoming the author of this book is fulfilling your mission and dreams on Earth? Can you see the book in your hands? Work on getting clarity... and then, keep writing!

Building Momentum in Your Writing

Once the introduction to your book is complete, you can begin filling in your chapters. It might take you some time to warm up, but once you do, you will be unstoppable. Writing a book is a little bit like riding a bike. First, you start off and you're wobbly. You feel like you're going to fall over. You crash into poles and gutters a few times and brush yourself off. You keep on trying, because you so badly want to ride that bike. And then, over time, the bumps and scratches heal, and you begin to fly down the streets, tackling bigger hills until you're flying down a mountain: free!

Give yourself the time and patience you need in order to generate your writing momentum. As you write, you'll begin to notice what your strengths are. You'll identify your struggles. You'll get to know more about what you need in order to write, and you will keep accessing it over and over again, as many times as you need to, to write the book. Your confidence will grow as you find yourself between pen and page. Be patient and persistent and you will soon be holding your book in your hands for the very first time.

You have now more than just begun your book: you are moving past the Introduction and creating the content for the chapters of your book. You are now immersed in the magic of book-writing and on the path to touching lives with your words. I commend you for finally beginning the journey of sharing what is inside your heart with the world: it is a journey few people start.

Chapter 7: The Writers Toolkit

"Good writing will bring you to places you don't even expect sometimes."

James Gandolfini

While writing an incredible book can rely on the author having a natural flair for the written word, there are also many strategies that authors can use to produce a book that is interesting and engaging, even to the point where the readers say "Wow" out loud while reading it. Despite varying from other books and being unique in its essence (providing that you write an original piece), the book that you write will incorporate one, more, many or all of the possible tools in what I call The Writers Toolkit. The Writers Toolkit consists of six core writing tools. While there are several smaller tools that can be applied, I want to focus on the common ones to give you the essential building blocks of creating a great manuscript. They are:

1. Stories (Storytelling)

2. Facts, Knowledge & Information

3. Quotes

4. Case Studies & Examples

5. Referencing – People & Content

6. Exercises

Each one of the above tools can contribute to a highly interesting book that impresses the reader. Each one can be used at different stages for different purposes. And, each one can be utilized towards the end outcome of communicating the message(s) in the book in the most potent way possible, so that the reader truly grasps what you are saying. This chapter will teach you how to incorporate one, two or all of these components into your book and do it well. There is a skill to each and knowing how to properly use the ones best suited to your book will assist you to improve your writing skills immensely. In this chapter, you will learn what each one is, what it is used for, and how to incorporate it into your book. Let's begin by talking about storytelling.

1. Story-Telling

Storytelling is a powerful way to communicate your message. It has been said that stories are a deeply effective method through which to educate and teach people. By their very nature, stories snag our attention and tend to make us curious. It could be said that hearing stories takes us back to fond memories of our childhood of being read to, either by a parent, carer or a teacher. We can both lose and find ourselves within stories, and so it is definitely wise to consider how you are going to use them to turn your manuscript into a masterpiece people can't put down, regardless of the genre.

A skilled story-teller speaking from stage can engage a room of thousands with a tale and hold their focus for hours. The same principle applies when you are working from the page with writing as your medium. You can hold someone's attention for days or even weeks on end through your storytelling ability as they make their way through your book. The more compelling the story the less likely someone is to want to put it down anytime soon. Before we explore what you can do to maximize your storytelling, let's talk about reasons why you might choose to incorporate stories into your book:

- To teach a point or principle

- To demonstrate a point or principle in a softer way

- To help the reader experience a realization about their situation in life without hitting them in the face with it

- To build rapport with the reader

- To make facts and knowledge more interesting

And now, let's talk about the art of writing stories well. I believe that in order to write a great story, you must do the following things:

- Present enough facts so the reader can follow the story

- Write the facts in an accurate manner (using real-life detail)

- Connect the dots from moment-to-moment without leaving the reader hanging

- Tell the story in a predominantly chronological format

- Use descriptive language to entertain the readers senses e.g. a crisp blue sky, a soft fluffy blanket, a fluoro green hoodie.

- Share how you / the person / people felt in the story

It's important to note here that storytelling is certainly not limited to fiction books. A powerful story can be one that is a real life story: for example, a story about a personal experience from either your own life or the life of one of your clients. Naturally, you will want to secure permission from each person whose story you would like to include or reference in your book *before* you use and certainly before you publish it. If you are going to utilize storytelling in your book – whether in part (for a few paragraphs) or in whole (the entire book e.g. a memoir) – then you may consider taking the following approach to begin writing it:

1. List out the five to ten main points that make up the basis of the story

2. Write the first draft of the story to connect and express these points

3. Review it and add in further descriptive language and feeling

I once heard a professional speaker say that "Facts tell, and stories sell" – and I agree. Stories have a powerful way of distracting the conscious mind so that the subconscious mind can absorb the value effortlessly and be remembered, in some cases, many years later. They shape and influence us in ways that other tools in The Writers Toolkit sometimes fail to do. Even a small handful of well-written stories can bring a book to life and make the words leap off the page.

2. Using Facts, Knowledge and Information

First of all, let me say that facts, knowledge and information are far more powerful than we may realize, as they are what provides the backbone for any decent book. In fact, these three components also provide the backbone for the stories within the book (notice above I talked about presenting facts in your stories). It could even be said that a great story is indeed the great presentation of a series of facts. Without any facts, knowledge or information, your book would have no depth to it. Even if you are writing a fiction book, the facts, knowledge and information you present in that book can still be highly educational for the reader. Take Dan Brown's book *The Da Vinci Code* as a prime example of this. Dan Brown utilized an enormous number of well-researched facts and information in his writing, around which he built the story for the book. The presentation of black-and-white information in your book can be made interesting through the following approaches:

- Linking them with a story

- Asking for the readers opinion/s

- Telling the reader how this helps them in their life (why it's important)

- Presenting them as a mystery that the reader needs to solve, or

- Sharing your own view on the information

Presenting facts, knowledge and information well is contributed to by your ability to organize your thoughts and ideas well into a logical order that makes sense to the reader. The simplest approach to doing this is to ask, "Which piece of information does the reader need to know first in order for the rest of the book to make sense?" You may even take your reader on a journey through the book by teaching them different levels of information about a topic from the simple (at the start) to the complex (in the later chapters). Or, you might present a series of facts as you step the reader through a 7-step system to (for example) empowering their relationship. Or, you might teach a range of content about your topic, just like I have done in this very book. All of the above are ways to empower and educate your reader. However you choose to present your facts, knowledge and information, the key is to be as clear as you can so that no 'loops' are left open by the time the reader reaches the final page.

Writing a book that presents a high level of information can require a greater degree of persistence, especially if you are still gaining clarity on what your method or body of work is. Writing an information-based book places you in the role of a teacher and the reader in the position of a student where they can learn something from you that could transform their entire life or their perspective on the world. It satiates the readers' desire for knowledge and will no doubt leave you with a greater appreciation of your brilliance than when you started writing.

3. Quotes

I am sure that you have, at some stage, picked up a book and noticed that the author has featured quotes within or at the beginning of their chapters. Integrating quotes into a book can give it more 'oomph', like adding herbs and spices to a dish. Including quotes, like the handful I have featured at the start of the chapters within this book, adds a different dimension to the book. You might view the quotes you use in your book as the back-up vocals for the main act (you). They give the reader something 'extra' to take away from your book.

The person you reference quotes from does not have to be famous. When I am searching for the perfect quotes to use in my manuscripts (which I usually do through our friend Google by typing in something like "quotes" and "leadership" in the search bar), I seek the perfect meaning to enhance the topic or message of that chapter or sub-chapter. Then, I simply reference the author. Now of course you might choose not to include a quote from someone because you don't agree with the person's morals or achievements, but that comes down to your personal judgment. I simply suggest choosing quotes that further enhance what it is that you have already said.

My suggestion around including quotes in your book is to search for unique quotes that aren't as commonly-used. I suggest digging up rarer quotes to exemplify the messages in your book, for the purpose of originality. I adore flicking through a book and finding quotes that I haven't heard before, where the author of the quote captured a deep meaning that I had felt but not yet been able to express.

4. Integrating Case Studies & Examples

The main purpose of using case studies and examples in a book is to assist the author to communicate the message more powerfully. This is not too dissimilar from the other five tools as they all aim to improve your written communication; however, a case study or example could be seen as a more direct method for backing up a point that you are trying to make. Books that teach the reader how to achieve a specific outcome tend to be the ones that feature a higher level of case studies and examples. For example, a self-development book written by a life coach may share case studies of their clients overcoming adversity by using their methods (with written permission, of course).

Case studies and examples can be used in numerous locations throughout a book, from the start of each chapter to the middle or the end of the chapter. The case studies and examples might be positioned with each step of a method as a way of showing the reader what the outcome could be possible for them if they apply it for themselves. In other instances, the book may present a point or method and then include a compilation of 'successful' case studies at the end of the book as an appendix: positioned as optional rather than mandatory reading.

The main challenge you may face when using case studies in a book is that they can be viewed as being "sales-y" e.g. the reader may feel that you are trying to sell or convince them of your message. However, there are also many people who find great value and satisfaction in knowing what results other people achieved or experienced by using a specific method. For case studies:

- Use high quality case studies with extreme or meaningful examples of results, achievement, etc.

- Don't overuse case studies within your text– unless the book is designed to be a compilation of case studies (e.g. a research piece)

- Present case studies and examples in a real and personal manner so the reader can relate to the human-ness of it

- Use examples from your own life – you are the author, after all!

- Introduce the case study/example in a way that catches the reader's attention e.g. open it with a question as opposed to "Here's a case study", which is an invitation for the reader to skip the next 500 words and resume reading after you've shared the example!

- For case studies about people, use personal language. For case studies about objects or non-human elements, more proper language may be appropriate.

Case studies and examples are often separated out from the body of text in the book by a 'box' with a light grey colouring for the background – or as italics – to contrast from the rest of the book. You do however have the option of integrating your examples into the text, weaving it into the main body of work. I suggest choosing your case studies wisely in terms of content and quality, and only using them when it is the most effective way for helping the reader to get the greatest benefit out of the book.

5. Referencing

Referencing other books, people or information can be a powerful way of adding a second or third viewpoint to your message. In essence, referencing the words or teachings of another individual (typically high profile ones) can add another dimension to the book. Referencing a person and information serves the purpose of showing the reader that what you are saying isn't necessarily uncommon knowledge. It could also be said that referencing others is a form of proof. You might notice that I have neatly referenced a few individuals throughout this book. I have done this in certain locations to build the power and credibility of what I wrote and show you that what I am teaching you has merit. You can reference content in many ways, including a single sentence, a quote (like we spoke about already), a paragraph, or an entire page of a book or article. Make sure that you do the following when referencing others:

- Give credit where credit is due: how would you feel if someone claimed the credit for your work?

- Thank the people you referenced in your acknowledgments (If you choose and depending how much content you referenced)

- Be clear on what is your opinion and what is their opinion

- Follow the applicable copyright laws for your city, state, and/or country

- Spell the person's name accurately (and the name of the article/book etc.)

- Use the references in appropriate places in your manuscript

Although referencing a third party can add power and credibility to your book, be careful not to overdo it. Referencing other people's bodies of work in every paragraph can leave the reader feeling that you don't have a voice as an author and that the book is more about other people's perspectives than your own. There is a fine line between enhancing your message with information from other people and drowning out your own message completely. Be conscious of this when you are including references to quotes, facts, and writings from people who you respect or admire and remember that you too have wisdom and knowledge worth sharing.

6. Creating Exercises for the Reader

Including exercises in your book is a powerful way to help the reader experience (not just read about) the value you offer. A well-placed exercise can give them an opportunity to put what you teach into action. You already aware by this stage that *The Book Within You* features a series of exercises that I have placed in relevant chapters and I included them for this exact reason: to help you write your book as you read this book. Like you do with your readers, I want to know that you can use what you learn.

The following is a list of ideas for exercises you could include in your book:

- Visualizations

- Step-by-step processes

- "Fill-It-Out" exercises

- Tick-boxes

- Choose-the-scenario (option a, b, c)

- Personality tests (etc.)

- Simple tips for what to do

- Exercises that leave lines below for the reader to write on

Exercises can be extraordinarily powerful as they allow you to reach out to the reader and make a bigger impact on their life. They provide the reader with a chance to act now and create what they want in their own life, whether that is to find a new relationship or grow their business to the next level. If the exercises you create are truly powerful, you will increase your chances of receiving raving reviews about your book. Here are my tips on featuring exercises in your book:

- Give clear instructions: there's nothing worse than confusing your reader

- Test each exercise out yourself to make sure it makes sense

- Break the exercise down into small steps so the reader can apply it

- Make sure the exercise matches the content you have paired it with

- Don't do overkill on exercises, unless your book is a workbook or designed to have a high number of exercises

- Use simple language when explaining the steps

- Make sure the exercises are well-formatted and laid out (visually)

When you are working on developing exercises for your book, try to generate original ones for the reader that they haven't done before. Spend a few moments or a few hours playing with different exercises. Apply them all yourself or test them with clients and potential readers before you add them to your manuscript. As the author, you want to know that your exercises work before you publish them in the book. Use yourself as a guinea pig: you might just make a discovery that changes your life and the lives of your readers.

I would love to challenge you now to work at least three of these writing tools into your book manuscript. Push yourself to work outside your comfort zone and find ways to improve your writing. Observe whether you prefer one of the tools over the others. Are you a natural story-teller? Do you find your flow when presenting a highly-technical piece? Or, do you enjoy referencing other gurus and leaders when you write? Whichever tools you prefer to work with, be open to adding to your repertoire as it may just take your writing to new heights.

Your Readers Can Feel You

The concept I am about to introduce is one of the most powerful pieces of advice I can give someone seeking to master the art of powerful writing. If you apply it, your entire experience of the written word will change forever and so will the reader's experience of your writing. The concept is this:

> How you feel when you write, is how the readers
> will feel when they read your writing.

Another way of explaining this is to say that how you feel while writing comes across in your words. Why? There are two explanations for this. The first is that how you feel impacts the words that you choose. E.g. if you are angry, you are likely to write shorter sentences with harsher language (or even use curse words). As another example, if you are sad, then you will tend to use words that reflect the sadness you feel. The second explanation is one that every word you write has an energy and vibration to it.

I believe that we are connected on a deeper level as human beings and that we have the ability to sense how someone else is feeling even if they are on the other side of the world. You might call it intuition or a connection with the collective consciousness, but it is undeniable that the words we speak and write impact those reading or hearing them. I love this concept because it holds the key to becoming an exceptional writer: to pay attention how you feel when you are writing. How you feel when you write is how your readers will feel on the other end. This means that you have the power to influence someone else's state of being through your own.

I can usually sense when one of my clients was upset or frustrated during their writing session when I'm reading their content. It comes across not just in the language they use, but in the overall feeling of the text. I can also tell if they were deeply inspired or in tears, because I will start to feel deeply inspired and tears will even well up in my eyes while I am reading. Writing is that powerful and this is what I want you to embrace on the deepest level possible. Pause for a moment and think about the energy you are putting into your book. How do you feel when you write? What state of mind have you been in when you sit down to work on your manuscript?

It's time to decide how you want your readers to feel when they are reading your book. Choose from and or circle feelings from the following list. You can also add one on the line below under "Other":

Uplifted	Powerful	Embraced	Nurtured
Inspired	Purposeful	Found	Curious
Grateful	Alive	Enthusiastic	Joyful
Hopeful	Relieved	Moved	Opened up
Awake	Vital	Energetic	Strong

Vulnerable	'Heard'	Significant	Beautiful

Other: _____

Every time you write, make a conscious effort to be in that state of being before you begin. Surround yourself with people, put yourself in places and fill your life with activities that create that state of being for you. And then, let the words pour out of you. The plus side of this (and this is life-changing if you get it) is that you will find yourself spending more time feeling the way you want to feel, not just how you want the reader to feel.! This is the beauty of the world and Zig Ziglar said it well: "When we help others get what they want, we get what we want." Writing for other people to help them feel uplifted will, in turn, uplift you. Writing to help other people feel empowered will, in turn, empower you.

There is one more note I would love to share before I wrap up finish this topic. I want you to tune in to how your writing feels to you, not just how it will feel to the reader. Start to notice when your writing gets too heavy: e.g. sad, sombre, depressing. Notice if your writing becomes angry: e.g. when you go on a rant. Remain aware of this as you write, because again, the voice that you put across in your manuscript will reflect the feelings within you. Focus on how you want your readers to feel at the end of your book. Get present with your message before you write. People will feel you speaking to them. They might even hear your voice in their head. They will feel your presence. They will feel as though you wrote the book just for them. This one insight can lead you to write a world-changing book.

Like any skill, mastery takes time. So, be patient with yourself as you find your feet as a writer. Continue to develop your skills and try out the tools that I have shared in this chapter. Find new ways to integrate stories, facts, knowledge, information, quotes, case studies, references and exercises into your book to make it the best book it can be.

Chapter 8: Winning the War on Writer's Block

"Don't wait time waiting for inspiration. Begin, and inspiration will find you."

H. Jackson Brown Jr.

One of the best demonstrations of a journey with writers' block I have seen is in the movie *Stranger Than Fiction*. If you haven't seen it, I apologize as I'm about to spoil part of the plot line for you. In the movie, the author (Karen Eiffel) is writing a novel about a character; and the character that she is writing about happens to be a real person – Harold Crick (played by actor Will Farrell) – whose life journey evolves in real time every time Karen writes the next part of the story. Karen experiences a severe case of writer's block as she tries to work out how to kill Harold Crick in her novel. She experiences every symptom of being "stuck" creatively all the way from snapping at people to smoking excessively.

A stubborn creature who is adamant that even her author assistant can't help her, Karen is featured in several scenes doing absurd things as she imagines the many different ways to kill the character at the end of the book: including sitting in the rain imagining cars driving off bridges into the river below and standing on the edge of the top floor of high-rise buildings imagining what it would be like to commit suicide. I won't tell you the ending, in case you haven't seen it, but I will say that Karen's writer's block dissolves in an unsuspecting moment when she walks out of a convenience store and sees an apple roll off the sidewalk onto the road, very nearly creating a traffic accident. And huzzah! Her writer's block ended, and she received her inspiration on how to kill Harold

Crick. And on that note, let's talk about you winning the war on writer's block should you face it on the journey.

Writer's block is typically referred to as the experience of sitting in front of a computer with a word document open and no words on the screen. To dissolve it, we first need to understand where it comes from, and this chapter will assist you to do exactly this. Before we go further, let me say that writing a book does take courage. Sitting and writing for long periods of time requires you to sit still and be present with yourself. It requires you to enjoy your own company; otherwise you're going to want to bolt at every chance you get, from the long hours required to bring your book to life. This is partly why writing is such a transformational experience, as it encourages us to face and get to know ourselves on a deeper level. May the next few pages enable you to overcome writer's block every time you come across it.

The Key Is in The Two C's

What is the key to becoming an unstoppable author? First, you must understand what the cause of writer's block is. As Albert Einstein once said, "A problem well stated is a problem half solved." In my experience, the primary causes of writer's block are:

1. Lack of **Clarity** (about the content or book)

2. Lack of **Connection** (to your content)

Let's explore these in detail now.

Clarity

A lack of clarity can occur around a number of things in a book, all the way from the outline to whether you have communicated the message effectively. It is, I believe, the primary source of writer's block. Every time you run into a part of the book where you aren't clear on what to do next, you run the risk of becoming 'stuck' or 'blocked'. Therefore, your ability to overcome writer's block relies on your ability to regain clarity as quickly as possible.

To reach a state of clarity and move forwards, you first need to identify what it is that you are stuck on. If it's the "whole book" you're struggling with, it indicates a lack of clarity with the book idea. In this instance, you may need to revisit the book in the Concept stage. Or, you might be stuck on which chapter should come before which, e.g. which is the correct order. During the writing process on my books, I often move my chapters around two or three times, and so it is quite natural to adjust them slightly as you write. To best approach to resolve a challenge of chapter order is to talk it out. Ask yourself which topic has to come first for the next one to make the most sense. In both of these examples, you have clearly identified what specifically you are stuck on and can now focus on resolving it.

Sometimes the fastest way to regain clarity on your book is to get as far away from it as possible. I have often walked away from my manuscripts for minutes, hours or a few days and come back with a fresh perspective. Sometimes all you need is a little distance: it's easy to become so close to the project that you are unable to see the answers.

Writer's block serves a purpose of helping you to improve the book. Every time you get stuck, identify the problem (what isn't clear) and find a solution for it, you can improve your book. If you have writer's block 20 times during writing your book, then you just improved your book 20 times. It's merely an opportunity to pause, reflect and improve before moving forwards. It could even be considered as a necessary part of the creative process as it helps you to refine your work.

Connection

I have coached people who are trying their hardest to write a book and they are simply not inspired enough to do it. They are, as general rule, not connected enough to the content they are writing about. In other words, it has little meaning to them. If this is you, I encourage you to reconsider whether the book you are forcing yourself to write is the one that you truly would love to write. And if it is, then I would suggest that you work on strengthening your connection to your content. Ask yourself, "How is writing this going to help me in future? How does it help me? Why does this inspire me?" You may also be lacking connection to the content you are writing because you are writing what you think you should be writing about your topic, not what you would love to write. The goal is to write the book that you are genuinely interested in writing as that will bring out your natural genius. Clarity on your book and connection to your content creates the feeling of inspiration, and inspiration leads to action.

Meaning First, Words Second

When people write, they are too commonly focused on the actual words. They worry about their grammar and punctuation and try their hardest to make it 'perfect'. But, unless you are now in the reviewing stage of producing the book, then you have your attention on the wrong thing. When I write, I focus on the meaning first, and the words second. It's essential that you know what you are writing about before you can how you will write about it. The words you use are a vehicle for communicating the meaning behind them; they are only there because of the meaning: the message. If I try to write something well but I have no idea what I am trying to say, I will feel frustrated. So:

Search for the meaning first, words second.

If you have ever experienced a moment of inspiration where words poured out of you, you will understand what I mean when I say that a strong connection to what you want to say automatically generates the desire to write. As you write your book, you will naturally uncover just how much depth is inside the body of work that you have (which could be your life story). And, the more depth there is, the more meaning you will find. Then, the words will fly out of you.

Chronological Writing

Contrary to what you might think, you don't have to produce your book in chronological order (from the first chapter to the last). Despite the fact that I tend to produce my Introduction first to set the foundation for the rest of the manuscript, I often move between topics and chapters when writing. I allow my inspiration to lead me to the chapter I feel like writing. As long as you have a strong, clear structure and outline for your manuscript and it is well-formatted ahead of time, you can take full advantage of the freedom to follow your bliss until the book is complete. So, create your structure and then move freely within it. Be flexible. If you are writing your life story, it does make sense to write chronologically as the story progresses, but in many cases, you can write your book out of order. My only advice is to ensure that the content all fits together neatly once you have finished so the book flows.

Deadlines or Dreadlines?

Some people function well under a deadline for writing their book and others feel that the pressure is too much and that it kills their writing spirit. When I know something has to be produced by the end of the month, it summons my writing energy and helps me to get into the zone. However, in other situations, I prefer to take my calendar and clock out of the equation completely. Which approach you choose depends on how you work as an individual. You may choose to set a deadline for business (e.g. make the book part of a marketing campaign) or for personal incentives (e.g. having the book written by Christmas so you can free yourself up and be with your family). It's entirely up to you. However, remember that a deadline can help you to stay focused and minimize distractions along the way.

Distractions

Many authors I coach are writing a book while also handling a full-time business or raising children. In their cases, it can certainly be more challenging to handle or manage the numerous distractions that can occur, especially when inspiration to write strikes. They might be in the middle of an important meeting or feeding their two-year-old when a brilliant idea arrives, and they can't write it down. What is the solution? Well, I believe that you have to fight for those moments. If you want your book to come to life, you've got to fight for it. You have to make it a part of your life. I know I certainly do. I can be in the middle of presenting a teleseminar and receive an idea for some content, and I would actually say it out loud or tell the participants, "I just got an idea for a book, please hang on while I write it down." and then I move on. I actually stop the world for my inspirations because I value them, and I know that they form my next book.

Writing your book is important: important enough for you to momentarily stop what you are doing and jot down the essence of what came to you. You don't have to write eight paragraphs to capture it, just write a few words to remind you about it later. My desk is often flooded with an array of colourful Post-It notes for that reason. I remember an experience not so long ago where I was getting a reflexology treatment on a Sunday morning. And, while I was being treated, a whole outline for a book (one that hasn't been written at the time of this books release) got downloaded into my mind. I kept emailing the notes to myself – right then and there – but the words just kept on coming. The therapist must have thought I was either an addicted socialite or workaholic as I laid there for 45 minutes typing on my phone. Make your book important and life will meet you halfway and help you produce it.

Shower Moments

This insight (which sounds sexy, I know!) about overcoming writer's block comes from one of my mentoring clients, Christie Pinto, author of *Who Has Got Your Back?* Throughout the writing of her book, Christie would run into questions that she had about one or many parts of her manuscript. And, she would routinely have what she called 'shower moments'. She would be stuck on something and then when she was in the shower, the answer would suddenly pop into her mind. I laughed many times working with Christie as she would start her sentence with, "So I was in the shower…" For Christie, her natural moments of clarity commonly occurred when she was alone in the shower. But, yours (because you do have your own version of shower moments) might occur in a different setting or place. Your shower moments might occur when you are driving, buying groceries, travelling, walking down the street, or working out at the gym. My shower moments occur when I am either in a conversation, doing self-development, on an airplane or listening to music.

Regardless of where and how your shower moments typically occur, they usually happen in a moment where you feel well, refreshed and present.

Anytime you aren't present, you are blocking your inspiration. But, if you're feeling grateful for your life and the people in it, you will experience a long line of shower moments. You do have the power to clear writer's block by changing your inner state of mind. I can induce an inspired writing state on almost any day if I look after myself both inside and out – and so can you.

10 Quick Ways to Win the War

Here is my short list on how to effectively win the war on writer's block:

1. Remind yourself of your vision

2. Pray to the heavens – ask the 'Universe' for help

3. Waste as little time as possible butting your head against the screen

4. Focus on the part of the book you *are* clear on

5. Get a good night's rest and come back to it in the morning

6. Write during the time of day/week where you are most inspired

7. Engage a book mentor/author trainer to guide you

8. Get connected to and interested in the content you're writing

9. Make plans for your book launch (covered later in the book)

10. Read earlier parts in the book to re-inspire yourself

The bottom line is: if you're sitting in front of a computer staring at a blank page waiting for the words to come and there's nothing there in that moment, it's not the best use of your time. It's actually okay to sit for a few minutes; the answer may bubble up if you are patient and still. But if you have spent more than 30 minutes staring at the screen, then I'd suggest getting off the computer and seeking an alternate strategy to overcome your writers block.

Writing Quotes to Inspire You

When all else fails, a solid quote about writing and books can provide you with what you need. You just never know who or what will 'unstick' you. Enjoy!

"In life, finding a voice is speaking and living the truth. Each of you is original. Each of you has a distinctive voice. When you find it, your story will be told. You will be heard."

John Grisham

"Authors like cats because they are such quiet, lovable, wise creatures, and cats like authors for the same reasons."

Robertson Davies

"Anybody who has survived his childhood has enough information about life to last him the rest of his days."

Flannery O'Connor

"A story is a letter that the author writes to himself, to tell himself things that he would be unable to discover otherwise."

Carlos Ruiz Zafón

"What really knocks me out is a book that, when you're all done reading it, you wish the author that wrote it was a terrific friend of yours and you could call him up on the phone whenever you felt like it. That doesn't happen much, though."

J.D. Salinger, The Catcher in The Rye

"Books are for nothing but to inspire."

Ralph Waldo Emerson

"A writer is someone for whom writing is more difficult than it is for other people."

Thomas Mann, Essays of Three Decades

"What I like in a good author is not what he says, but what he whispers."

Logan Pearsall Smith

"All artists' work is autobiographical. Any writer's work is a map of their psyche. You can really see what their concerns are, what their obsessions are, and what interests them."

Kim Addonizio

"Fool! Nothing but black ink runs through my veins!"

Hiromu Arakawa

"Writing is.... being able to take something whole and fiercely alive that exists inside you in some unknowable combination of thought, feeling, physicality, and spirit, and to then store it like a genie in tense, tiny black symbols on a calm white page. If the wrong reader comes across the words, they will remain just words. But for the right readers, your vision blooms off the page and is absorbed into their minds like smoke, where it will re-form, whole and alive, fully adapted to its new environment."

Mary Gaitskill

Writing a book is not supposed to be a hard slog. It's an opportunity for you to share what you believe in. It's important that you don't view writer's block as a challenge that threatens the success of your book. It is merely an indicator that something isn't clear about your book, that you are temporarily disconnected from your vision, or that your focus is in the wrong place for the words to flow readily. Every case of writer's block can be dissolved if you are determined enough. So, have a strong enough reason to overcome it. Be deeply enrolled enough in the end outcome of you becoming a published author that you are relentless when it comes to solving problems, figuring out a new strategy, and overcoming obstacles. Don't let a momentary bout of struggle and beating your head against a wall defeat your entire dream. Win the war on writer's block.

Chapter 9: The Art of Channelling

"Fill your paper with the breathings of your heart."

William Wordsworth

C hannelling is a topic I have been asked about many times in the past decade. People want to know how to tap into that illuminating state of mind where the words pour out onto the page: that inspiring experience where books can be written in a matter of days and where it feels as though the words flow through you from a higher source. As you know from earlier in the book, I experienced the magic of channelling when I wrote my book *The Inspirational Messenger* over the Easter weekend in 2013. On the Tuesday night before the weekend, I had a strong sense that I would be writing a book that weekend. I felt it from deep within me. When the feeling came over me, I thought, "Really? I just finished writing my last book and it hasn't been released yet." But, the urge from within my soul was stronger than any doubts I had about whether it was possible to write a book in four short days.

On the Thursday evening, I began to plan the outline for the book (step two of the journey). I wasn't crystal clear what the book would be about initially. However, as I spent three hours mapping out the content of the book, I identified that there would be five pillars and that the book would fulfil two purposes: inspiring the reader and guiding them to become inspirational in everything they do (in other words, to make a meaningful difference in the world). I could feel the book bubbling up from deep within me and from far beyond me. I had already cleared my schedule for that weekend, and so the following morning, I woke up early, sat down on the couch in my office, and started writing. I barely moved until midnight. Thousands and thousands of words poured out of me that day: a phenomenon that continued to occur for the next three days. I wrote for more than 12 hours every day over the weekend. By the time Monday evening arrived, the book manuscript was 51,000 words in length and nearly complete. On the Saturday alone, I wrote a whopping 12,000 words.

There is no doubt that I was channelling that weekend. When I began, I wasn't sure what would come out of me or which direction the book would go in; I just knew that it was time for it to be written and that I was the one destined to write it. At the beginning of the weekend, I had turned my head upwards to the heavens and said a prayer: "If writing is my greatest gift, then allow this book to demonstrate that." My prayer was answered and fulfilled beyond my wildest imagination. I could have channelled a single message, a page, a blog or an entire book that weekend. I didn't know where it would go when I began. I just knew it was in the hands of the divine, and at that particular moment, I was the vehicle for the book to become manifest in the world.

When you are channelling words onto the page, your conscious mind takes a backseat. Your human brain no longer becomes a control centre, but more so a vehicle that enables and allow the writing to happen. Your mind becomes present as the inner chatter is silenced by the presence of a greater message. Channelling can be an experience that evokes deep healing as bringing inspiring writing to life on the page uplifts you in the process. It is for this reason that channelling is one of my favourite ways to write, whether that writing is for a book, article, or a social media post.

When words begin flowing to you in this state of mind, they are often accompanied by a sense of urgency to find pen and paper and capture what is being given to you. It's as though your heart and soul want to escape from within you and run free on the pages. Your body becomes animated by inspiration. It feels like the sentences are writing themselves. You don't know what words will come next, but you just know that they will – and they do, every time. While channelling, you open up to what is within your heart and soul. Time and space disappear. Whatever is happening in your life ceases to exist for a moment. It is common for writers who have had encounters with the magic of channelling to say, "It doesn't feel like I wrote that."

I have a range of different experiences when I channel. Sometimes, I hear the words in my mind before I put them down on paper. Other times, I hear the words just a few seconds before or while I am in the process of writing them. The voice rarely sounds like someone I know (in fact, I don't think it ever has); it usually sounds like myself but many years in the future. Other times, I feel the sensation within me that I want to write and when that happens, I find the empty page and just write. I surrender to the process and watch the words appear on the page in front of me. In this chapter, I will endeavour to assist you to experience this for yourself.

Before I do, I want to explain the difference between channelling and automatic writing. For me, channelling is where you tune into a much higher, divine force – call it your soul, the universe, the collective consciousness – and the words appear to come to you. You become the messenger for a meaningful message. On the other hand, automatic writing (to me) is not necessarily a style of writing that involves an access to one's soul. You can perform automatic writing where you simply write out what is on your mind and experience writing flow while doing so. When you are channelling, you don't always know what the next words will be until they are down on the page. However, when you are engaged in automatic writing, you tend to know what you are about to write before you write it. Channelled writings have an inherent power to them, which words written in any other way may not have and the experience of producing them is deeply enriching. It gives you the sensation that you truly are part of and one with something greater: what you might call, the divine order of the universe we live in.

Your Relationship to The Divine

What I love about channelling is that, over time, it can bring about deep and lasting change in your life. Channelling guides you to connect with a 'greater force' to write the most inspiring words possible. In connecting with your soul and the universe at large, you also connect with this same guiding force for every other area of your life. It's entirely possible that while you are channelling your book you will also receive ideas for your business or insights for your relationships.

Because you rarely know what is going to appear next on the page while channelling, it requires you to let go and trust in the greater perfection that is at work in the universe. Channelling, not unlike writing in general, is a process of exploration, and in order to explore new oceans, we must be willing to let go of the shore. Trust that God, the universe, and the divine order is the artist, you are the paintbrush and the page is the canvas. Allow yourself to be moved, called and guided to create your book. Exploring your relationship with the divine order of the universe through experiences like channelling unleashes magic from within you.

The pen and paper is a safe space. The page is not going to judge you. So, trust yourself to sit in front of a blank page and have 'God' speak through you; to guide your hands to write a message of inspiration. Develop the faith that you are not in this world or life alone. You can tune into your soul any moment you choose. Your confidence will grow over time; and suddenly, words will ask to be written through you. They will choose you as their messenger: the person who has been chosen to deliver inspired teachings to the world in the form of a published book.

You do have the ability to tune into a higher frequency. You can hear, see and write more powerful words. Let them flow through you. Your higher self (your soul, your spirit) is massless, timeless and boundless. It is infinite. You are here on Earth to express your greatest potential in every way you would love, and channelling accelerates that process. It enables you to create and strengthen that channel and relationship with and to the divine, so that you can access it regularly and great works can come through you for the world to read.

Clearing Your Channel

Before I reveal insights about how you can develop your channelling ability, I want to start by exploring some of the things that commonly stop us from channelling. You might or might not relate to these in your own life. I share them to help you examine your relationship with writing and channelling more deeply. The end outcome is that you can, of course, access the mystical state of being where you become a writing machine. I want to begin by exploring the concept of giving and receiving.

I have observed many people struggling to receive openly, whether that is money, relationships, opportunity, and a more rewarding experience of life. Well, channelling while writing is the ultimate receivership. It challenges us to allow the words and the energy they bring to come through us. We don't have to work for it: it just arrives. It's a gift from the heavens. When we allow the words to come through us, it strengthens our relationship with ourselves and increases our sense of self-worth. It leads us to feel over time that we are worthy because we have been given something great – the gift of beautiful words – and therefore we are destined to do something great in the world.

Your 'blocked pipe' around channelling may also reflect your relationship with yourself. As channelling is one of the purest experiences a person can have, you may struggle if you are beating yourself up putting pressure on yourself to be someone you aren't. Remember: you are magnificent and appreciate that there are no mistakes in life. The greatest truth a human being can accept is the knowing that everything on the outside that happens around them is connected to something – an emotion, memory or feeling – on the inside. And when the inside changes, so does the reality that they find themselves immersed in. If you feel stuck on the outside, reflect inwardly on where you feel stuck inside. This applies when writing your book: if you feel stuck when writing, it is time go within and find a solution to your inner world first. Until you do, channelling isn't likely to occur.

Letting your ego run the show can also hinder your channelling ability. You may be fighting against the greater perfection of life, thinking that you know better than the universe does, and that life ought to happen your way. The channelling then becomes a game of power where you try to control when you will channel as opposed to becoming open and humble to the message you are here to share with the world. One of the most fulfilling experiences I know is to write for the simple reward of writing, and to allow the outer rewards like book sales and accolades to come naturally, regardless of whether you channelled your book or not. Acknowledge the source; the higher power; both within you and beyond you. Work with it in your book and your life. There is no need to try and win. There is no race you have to come first in. To channel is to understand that you are a channel for the information or wisdom that comes through you. In fact, I'm sure that is why it is called 'channelling': because you become a channel while doing it.

Accessing Your Channelling Ability

Let's explore what you can do to begin tapping into your channelling ability. You first of all must start out with the desire to channel: that is essential. Then, come to appreciate the miracle of channelling, understanding that the most sacred of teachings, wisdom and knowledge can come to and through you when you are channelling. It is truly a mystical experience where you may feel as though you have been given access to privileged information: because you have. Appreciate how it will inspire you in the process. And finally, appreciate the state of perfection that you will see and feel when the words land perfectly on the page.

You are going to develop a new relationship with yourself, with life, and with the divine. You are about to reach out and up to the heavens and trust that 'someone' will be there for you – and not just once, but every time. You will learn that you are safe in life. You will discover what the message of your life is and reunite with your soul. And now, let's talk about the five things you can do, think and feel to increase the chances of channelling while you write your book.

1. Strong Book Concept & Outline

Two of the essential preparations for channelling have already been addressed by the time you are reading this chapter: the book concept and outline. When you are clear on the topic, direction and angle of your book and you can see how the content will flow, it opens a direct path between you and the heavens.

2. Harness the Power of Your Challenges

Many people don't know this, but two weeks before I channelled and wrote *The Inspirational Messenger*, I had experienced a relationship break-up. At the time (before I appreciated that it really was time for us to move on and thus our break-up was a blessing), it felt like someone had slapped me across the face. There is no doubt that I was hurting that weekend. I was wondering what the future had in store for me and whether I would find deep love with someone again.

I believe the emotional chaos which was bubbling away under the surface provided me with fuel for writing 51,000 words in four days. I wanted to avoid my pain and so, I ran to the place of safety I knew would forever be there for me: the pen and page, my words, and writing. I buried myself in my laptop for four days seeking healing – and I found it. The experience of writing that book was profound and special to me and still is today. It helped me through a tough time by giving me a way to connect with my heart and soul and remember who I really am. The adversities you have faced in your life can help you heighten your experience of writing: so, embrace them.

3. Create a Clear Space for Yourself (And the Words)

I try to create an inspiring environment for myself whenever I intend to channel. This might come in the form of a week away, a few late-night writing sessions, or scheduling out every Saturday in my calendar for six weeks until I've finished my book. Do the same for yourself. Set up an environment – a space, place and time – for yourself in which you will begin to explore your ability to channel inspired writings onto the page. Clear your mind as well as time in your calendar. Allow yourself the space to open up and allow the universe to speak through you. I listen to music that uplifts me when I write and begin to channel. If you do listen to music, make sure that it inspires, enlivens and moves you. It can assist you to access that space within you where the words are.

4. Realize That Now Is the Perfect Moment

Channelling can be unpredictable and despite the fact that I am teaching you a few tips right now on how to channel, I also believe it is largely in the hands of the greater perfection of life when it occurs. I imagine sometimes that the divine order is making sure the world is never missing all the books that humanity needs at that one moment in time and that as soon as a new book is needed to help humanity, someone will be assigned the task to channel it into manifestation.

5. Send A Prayer to The Heavens/God/Universe

The fifth insight that will empower you to awaken your channelling ability is to do what I did when I channelled *The Inspirational Messenger*: send a prayer to the heavens, God, or universe before you begin (whichever one suits your religious and spiritual perspectives on life). Although I too have had my cynicisms at times about why things happen the way they do, at my core I am certain that there is a loving, intelligence all around and within us and that we can work with and access it when we write. Don't be afraid to send or write an inspired prayer: it might just bring an incredible work through you.

You can channel anywhere, anytime, on any day of your life. There are no set rules. It is a gift that is available to you 24 hours a day. I first started channelling when I was still in school wearing a uniform and being graded on my intellectual capacities. I didn't have money, a job, business or social significance. I wasn't sitting on a mountaintop in the Alps or in a sacred temple in India. I've channelled in airports, on planes, in cafés, sitting up in bed at night, at my desk, and even while driving (yes, I know, it's extremely dangerous and I don't recommend it). Your intention to channel is half the journey. People don't always ask to begin channelling – their life leads them to it. but, there is no reason that you can't set the intention to experience it, for yourself and the world.

When words come into your mind, write them down and follow your intuitive urges on what to write next. Follow the yellow brick road. Continue opening up. Open up again. Melt into the words. Melt again. Life and writing aren't always about control and channelling requires the least control of many of the things you will do in your life. So, enjoy it. Embrace it. Welcome it. Love it. Follow your bliss. Follow the words bliss. Ask the heavens what message you are here to bring to Earth and then rise to the top of your industry by bringing through a book that is unparalleled.

It's entirely possible that the purpose of channelling while writing is to allow people a connection to the higher level of who they are and to show them just how infinite their potential is. It gives us a direct access to the soul and beyond. If you want to be successful as an author, you will want to create a book unlike any other. And, if you are setting out to do this, then it's imperative that you connect with your most authentic self: who you truly are.

Channelling helps you to do exactly that. In reverse, it's not possible to tune into who you really are without somehow being guided to an elevated experience of writing (assuming that writing a book is something that is within your heart). Every person has the capacity to channel when writing. The deeper you go into the content in your book, the more you will discover what you didn't know that you knew. And, if you love your book enough, the topic will reveal all of its secrets to you and bring you to this effortless, mystical experience of writing.

Chapter 10: Turning Life Adversities Into Written Legacies

"There is a book within every chapter of your life."

Emily Gowor

O ver the years, I have worked with many people who want to share their life story in a book. This desire is often stirred by the fact that people have been through extraordinary challenges in the past and, having come through it to the other side, they now want to share that tragedy-to-triumph story to empower other people to overcome the adversities they face. When they discover their desire to share their story, it is usually accompanied by an overwhelming sensation that it 'has' to be written: that there is so much inside of them they want to let out. In some cases, the drive becomes so strong that nothing will stop them from expressing themselves.

Mentoring people to write their life stories has become a bit of a niche for me over the years, as so many people seeking to publish their story have sought my guidance to assist them on the journey. I have been blessed to provide a safe space and heartfelt encouragement for them: one in which they can shine light on their past for the world to benefit from. In reading people's stories, I have been deeply moved by the wisdom that is within us and how resilient we truly are. Turning your life story into a written legacy is not just about pouring your past onto the page – a cathartic experience – but it truly can provide much-needed inspiration for other people.

So, let's talk about sharing your story. The doubt that people often feel when setting out to write their story sounds something like this: "Who cares about my story? Why would people read it?" First of all, let me ask you this: Have you considered, instead of who wouldn't read it, who *would*? What about your children? What about your family? What about your friends? What about your clients? Focusing on who won't read your book is like focusing on your weaknesses. Start with who you know the book will help and work on it until you establish certainty on who your target readers are.

The success of a memoir-style book does depend on how the book is positioned and marketed. For this reason, I suggest identifying the niche of your life story before you begin writing. For example, you might be a woman who overcame a tricky divorce and rebuilt yourself financially from the ground up. This life story may be told and then marketed with that point of view, with the target reader being other women who have come out of a relationship financially destitute. The angle here is women and finances. This particular memoir could serve as an inspirational story to help women move forwards. Another example of a memoir may be a businessman's journey of making a mint, losing it, and making it back. This life story would typically be of interest to entrepreneurs. It's all in the positioning: a great title, cover and clear niche can work wonders in capturing the attention of potential readers.

What to avoid when it comes to turning your journey into a book is the tendency to just open up a word document and go "blah" where you dump your entire life story onto paper *without* giving any consideration to the end product. Give thought to what kind of life story yours is, even if you're not planning to write a memoir-style book. It's also important to realize that your one life story might speak to different niches; for example, my own life story could be positioned towards aspiring authors as I share the twists and turns of my journey with pen and page. Or, it could be written from the perspective of being a young female entrepreneur and marketed to other young entrepreneurs.

If you are still in doubt about the sell-appeal of your life story as a book, then I also suggest shifting the style of your book slightly and doing what several of my clients have done: blend other mediums from the writers' toolkit together with your life story. You might opt to tell your story in the first half of the book and then share a method in the second half. You might include images, exercises, affirmations, and so on to give the reader huge value from the book. Or, you can let the story stand strong on its own and then produce a second or third book of a different nature where it is all about teaching and empowering the reader. Regardless of whether you choose to do this or not, I suggest taking a moment to become present with the value in your story. Look inside your heart and remember that we are all human: because of this, there is incredible value in hearing about the life experiences of another human being.

We all have a story worth telling, sharing, and reading. It's not essential for you to have climbed Everest, made a million dollars or saved another person's life in order to have a life of meaning. We can be too superficial sometimes about what it is that we think makes a "good" life story. We think it has to be movie-worthy for it to be interesting at all. You can have what you might consider a more average existence and still draw significant value from it by being a deep thinker or by overcoming challenges that humanity faces. It all depends on your attitude towards your life and how much you believe that every day of your life is full of wisdom that can be learned and shared.

It is sometimes the quiet achievers, not those who tower above others in terms of success, that have the most moving stories. I know many people who would love for their parents to write a book, because they want to know how their parents saw the world or what life was like when they were young. Many of the great leaders in business and self-growth share the 'shine' of the diamond without revealing the truth about how they got to where they are in a way that others can relate to it. They hide it. Sharing your story in detail can give people a roadmap to their own success if you are willing to share it.

You don't have to go through what someone else has in order to relate to it – and the same applies with your readers to you. We all have experiences of life that no one else on this planet has had. No one is exempt from challenge in this world: we are in it together as human beings. Sharing your life story is about documenting it – raw and real – and then getting it into the hands of people who need it: people who are now at where you once were. It's about making sure they don't feel alone when they face adversity. It is to show them that someone has made it through, which could be all the strength they need to get through it themselves. That is leadership; helping people to rise up and being there in the tough times, even in the form of a book. I commend every person who shares their life story in this way, because there is no doubt that it takes an enormous amount of courage to reveal yourself to the world.

Life Adversities Make Great Stories

It has to be said that life adversities often make interesting stories. I have read several books, particularly those of my clients, where the author shared the intimate details of their upbringing and it was both entertaining and moving. I've had many teary moments grasping the intensity and depth of the author's experience and, in many cases, am deeply moved by the immense courage and character it took from them to overcome it. The stories have involved extreme sexual promiscuity, beating, depression, anxiety, relationship break-ups and make-ups, failure, divorce, death and more. They have revealed a personal journey of what millions of people are dealing with on a daily basis and given a voice to those other millions through the story.

A client once asked me how many of my own personal adversities I have shared. My answer? I have written about some of them, but there are certainly stories that are yet to make it into the light. In many of my writings, I have shared the experience of overcoming depression at age 19 and finding my purpose and calling in life. I share the journey of building a future for myself from the ground-up. Over the years, other stories will come out. I will share each one with a specific purpose. Here's why: When you are writing and sharing a personal story, it is wise to be conscious of how telling that story will position you in the marketplace and world, especially if you have a business or want to use your book to grow your business. For example (and this is an extreme example for the sake of the principle), if you share a story about overcoming rape, you may become known as "the girl/guy who overcame rape". Depending on how intense your story is, it may linger in people's minds for years to come.

This is perfectly fine in cases where you are helping women and men to overcome their own sexual adversities through coaching, speaking and workshops, or if you are teaching relationship and tantric work, for example.

In fact, in this case, it will actually do you a great service and it will certainly get media attention. However, if you are a corporate consultant, the publishing of a book like this may have ramifications that you will need to address. I'm not saying don't reveal your story: I'm just making sure that you do it consciously and with a clear intention in mind. You can just choose to open up and share the gory details but do it with an end goal in mind.

When I share the part of my life where I was laying on the floor wanting to take my life at age 19, I do it because it is the perfect foundation from which to then teach people about living an amazing life. I also know that a majority of people have had a similar experience at some point in their lives. I know that thousands or millions of people can personally relate to the moment where you are driving down the highway and think about running the car into a concrete barrier out of desperation. I was blessed that I overcame depression, however I know that many people are still living in apathy about the future. It's my mission to inspire them to get up off the floor and plan their life so they can discover just how fulfilling being alive can be. I share the story openly because it is the part of my life journey that assists me with my mission to bring not just books, but inspiration, to the world. Who could your story inspire?

When Is It Story-Time?

> "The role of a writer is not to say what we can all
> say, but what we are unable to say."
>
> *Anais Nin*

Some personal life stories are written at the time when the person is encountering it (like a diary, if you will) and other stories are told in past tense. And yet, neither one is better than the other. They are simply two different ways of writing your story. Some people naturally assume that it's best to tell a personal story once the person has already overcome it whereas other people prefer to read the person's encounter with adversity as they are experiencing it, as though it was live. Which one do you prefer? Your answer to this question may determine the approach that you will take with your own story. Of course, if you have overcome your adversity or it happened several years ago, you will write it in past tense by default. However, for those of you who are currently experiencing your life-altering moments, let's briefly explore the upside and downside of both approaches so you can make an informed decision about how you are going to write your story.

Writing in the Moment

When you document your story as you are living it, you are more likely to increase the chances of capturing raw feeling and emotion on the page: because it's real, right now. You might relate to the experience of writing a piece and then reading it weeks or years later and thinking, "Wow!" because what you wrote was so raw. Even if you don't publish your story immediately (because you will need to choose the moment at which the story and the book ends, too), using fresh content like this in the book can deeply move the reader and allow them to feel what you feel, as you felt it. This could prove to be very powerful if you are on a healing journey, for example. The reader will be able to heal with you as they read your story. The book will become a vehicle for them to move on: when you move on, so will they.

When we are in the present moment with an experience, we are strongly associated into the 'now'. All of our senses are heightened. This means we can capture more of the sensory details of our experience – smell, taste, sight, sound, and touch – which typically leads to a more engaging story when it's captured in writing. We also tend to remember more of the finer details about what is occurring now than we sometimes do when ten or thirty years have passed, and so, capturing it now can provide you with ample content to draw on later when you work on creating your book. I am making notes ahead of time for my autobiography to ensure that I capture more of the finer details for my readers, being well aware that I may not appreciate the importance of this moment I'm in right now as much later on once I've grown through it.

The downside of writing your story as you go, is that any emotions you haven't yet made peace with can make their way onto the page, which may or may not actually be useful for the reader. Your book might sound a bit more like a highly-emotional, passionate, upset rant than an inspiring and deeply moving piece. I place additional caution on this when the client I'm coaching is a life coach themselves or positioning themselves as a leader in personal transformation. If you want to attract and generate more clients through your book, the content in the book will need to demonstrate to the reader that you walk your talk and that you can assist them to change their own life. If you sound chaotic and emotional throughout the book, they are less likely (as a general rule) to trust in your skills. Be aware of this as you write, and you can still manage to capture the emotion in-the-now while also uplifting and guiding the reader to make an affirmative change in their own life.

Looking Back on It Now

Naturally, the upsides and downsides of writing a life story once you have already lived through are almost the reverse of what we explained about writing it in the moment. Writing a story several months or years after it has occurred e.g. sharing a childhood story when you are now 40, has power in the sense that you are likely to have now made something of yourself, and at the very least, made different choices about your life. It's more likely that your story will read like a rags-to-riches or tragedy-to-triumph story guaranteed to encourage the reader to dream big and follow the same path for themselves. Although this type of story is quite common, I still believe there aren't enough of them in the world. We all need encouragement from time-to-time in the form of a story that makes us want to rise up from the ashes and conquer our nemesis, whatever that might be.

In having the time to reflect on your adversity from the past, you are likely to have drawn a long line of life lessons from them – or even one strong, core message – that you can now fill the pages of your book with. Your memoir now becomes an intriguing self-help book for others to draw wisdom from, and you become a leader in that sense. You are lifting others up by showing them how far you have come and what you have learned along the way.

The downside of capturing your story once you have already been through it is that, once you have emotionally 'processed' the feelings that you encountered at the time – and the impact that it had on you – you can sometimes lose the original impact that the story had. I personally have found blessings in so many of my earlier life experiences that the original drama and emotion has dissolved, and I see them differently, sometimes to the point where I don't see a purpose in sharing it with others. The bigger the challenge was at the time, the more connected you will be to it even after emotionally-processing of the story, so writing it later on doesn't necessarily mean that you lose the impact: it is just something to be aware of when writing your story in past tense. When you write, reflect on how your life was at the time, the people who were there, what you were wearing and how you felt, and bring as much of the detail forwards to engage the reader as you tell your story.

Regardless of the approach you take to sharing your life story, you are likely to encounter healing as you write it. Writing your life's journey will help you to reconcile the past so that you can move forwards into a new future for yourself. One of the most powerful ways to do this is to find the blessings that came out of the circumstances that once challenged you. The following topic has been designed to help you with this.

Finding Gold in The Mud

Finding the gold in the mud is about changing your perception of the past through understanding that no matter what happens to you (or what you do), there is a greater reason for it. There is a blessing hiding inside every circumstance. I haven't yet met someone who hasn't faced obstacles or who has been exempt from challenge: we all have it. We've grown up without parents, been in tough relationships, failed at something, and felt lonely, insignificant, unattractive and rejected. But, it is these very same adversities that drive us to be great, and these experiences may very well inspire you to write a book to help others overcome them, too. Ask the following questions when you are faced with challenges in your life:

- What quality in me is this challenge developing? E.g. strength, maturity

- What am I learning from my life today?

- What opportunity or insight is this circumstance trying to show or give me?

- How is this crisis a blessing?

If you transform your greatest problems by seeing how they are helping you become who you were born to be, you will transform your life. In moments of challenge in my life today, I think, "This is preparing me because there is something greater ahead." And it's true. I choose to see life that way. When I was a child, I felt rejected at school; I didn't fit in with the "cool" kids. I had two close friends (give or take one) throughout most of my school years. You only have to take one look at my life today to see how far that one childhood wound has driven me. It has moved me to do great things, propelled me to take a stand for what I believe in I also felt like I couldn't communicate as a teenager. I began talking to myself... on paper. That was the start of my writing career. Would I trade in finding my gift for an easier upbringing? Not a chance. It, amongst several other adversities, has shaped me into who I am today and who I will become in the future. Appreciate the role that your pain has played for you, too. Your toughest times are what have shaped you into the incredible human being that you are.

The Risks and Rewards of Bearing Your Soul

It's time to explore the risks and rewards of publishing your life story. Let's begin with the risks.

RISKS

People who turn their life story into a book often experience doubts that sound like this: "My friends don't know that about me," or "What will my family going to think if they find out what I went through?" These are concerns that it is important to address before you begin writing: because it's true, people will be impacted when they learn intimate details about you that you haven't shared before. This particularly applies in cases where you have experienced 'abuse' (sexual, physical, etc.) or other extreme experiences, and even more strongly where you are writing about a person (the perpetrator, for example) who is still alive when you publish the book. It is also important to know that most publishing houses won't release a work where the author attacks another person as it is considered to be libel and can invite legal issues later down the line. Bear this in mind when you share your story.

Some people will feel the fear of being vulnerable and exposed and share their story anyway, knowing that it will stir people up as much as it will inspire. Their philosophy is usually along the lines of, "This is my story, and this is who I am. It's time to come out." Sharing your story can be a deeply freeing experience. Other people will release their book under an alias, which avoids the potential ramifications but also means you will miss your chance to achieve credibility with the book's release.

One of the other risks that you run in sharing your story relates to the mentioning of other people in the book. This comes down to ethics. This will always be a case-by-case issue, where whether you acquire verbal or written permission from a person to mention them in the book will be dependent on the nature in which you wrote about them. For example, if you are sharing the gory details of an event in your life and that involves sharing the details about someone else too, I would ask the person before publishing them in your book. In fact, I tend to be highly conscious of mentioning other people in my books and will tend ask the person even if I experience a gut instinct that says it wouldn't be okay to publish it without written permission. This also applies when the story edifies the person or affirms their work. You just never know: they may be uncomfortable with you publishing information about them in your book.

A number of psychologists and counsellors will often reference client case studies in their books through changing names and details of the people involved. This is fine; however, I apply the same principle of ethics and encourage them to ask the client for their permission regardless, as it's easy for a client to read the book later on and know that story was about them. Place yourself in the shoes of the person you are writing about before you decide to publish their name and mention without their permission. Again, the one thing that I tell my clients in this instance is, "If in doubt, ask." If the person has passed on, it is slightly different. You may choose to mention them anyway (say if they are your parents) or you might choose to talk to the people close to them about it. Use your intuition in each case. Regardless of what you choose to do in each situation, the risks of turning your life story into a book can all be addressed and overcome, and my suggestion is to work through them if you have your heart set on including your story in your book.

REWARDS

The greatest reward of bearing your soul is the sheer strength that it brings you: both in having the courage to open up and bear all and in allowing yourself to be a guiding light for other people. When I share my story of being on the floor at age 19, its still feels raw to me at times, but the comfort and strength I need comes in knowing how many people need to know that an extraordinary life is possible and depression doesn't have to be the end of the road.

Writing your story is rewarding in that it also invites you to get to know yourself on a deeper level. If you are upset with someone, you write your story and they are in it, it's likely going to come out. It will be an opportunity for you to examine your feelings and put the past into a new perspective. Your life is your life: it is the most precious asset that you have, and so writing a story about it is naturally going to be a very deep experience. It will make you revisit what you haven't loved, stare your demons in the face and grow as a human being. And, on the flip side, it will lead you to celebrate the amazing moments. It is about bearing the whole of who you are: and loving yourself and your journey of life regardless.

I love it when people say, "I've been holding my story inside me for years and I'm ready." Their life has now led them to a place where they want to inspire others and help people get more out of life. This is another great reward of bearing your soul. While it may challenge the people closest to you to learn things about you that they realize you hid from them, in the long run it's likely to build the relationship to be even stronger. Bearing your soul will have your clients and people in general feel closer to you; because they now know what you have been through as well as why you do what you do.

What's on The Other Side of Your Story?

An amazing phenomenon occurs once you have written a book that expresses your story. I've witnessed this in myself and in a portion of the people I have coached on their writing journey. And it is this:

> Once you write your story, your body of work begins to emerge.

When you share your story with people, you will often experience a sense of completion with your journey through life. A healthy detachment occurs between the author and what happened in the past. This can be incredibly powerful. I even had a client who said she got bored of her story once she wrote it and she now wanted to focus on teaching clients rather than telling them about her life, which was a long way from where she was when she began writing the book! When we are going through a challenging time, we often have a desire to be heard and felt – to be understood – and to finally get the story off our chest. So, having someone else read and acknowledge all that we have been through can be an inspiring experience. What emerges on the other side writing a life story is usually clarity about several things:

1. Who you are

2. What your purpose and mission is

3. What business you'd love to run or career you'd love to have

4. Who and what is most important to you

5. What you want to help other people with

When the clarity arrives, it can become the starting point for a body of work or a mission in the world. Or, it brings a new methodology or therapeutic process. Or, a whole new life plan appears for the author. All of these are equally powerful to one another. I have found that in most cases that people move on with their life in a powerful way once they share their story, because they now have closure on the past and can venture boldly and without restraint into the future. They said what they wanted to say, felt what they needed to feel, and they put the past on the shelf with love and grace. So, you just never know: life after publishing your story may be very different and not just because you are now a published author.

Your life story doesn't stop until the day that you do. Even once you have passed over from this life, you story can and will live on. You can become published, touch lives, and be acknowledged for who you are. You can grow your business through sharing where you have come from. You can provide people with the inspiration to follow their dreams. Life stories are a powerful medium. Being alive as a human being is a full-immersion experience from which you can draw many pearls of wisdom to help humanity. Remember, we're all in this together.

Chapter 11: Mindset = Manuscript

"If you can dream it, you can do it."

Walt Disney

It's my intention that by this stage of reading *The Book Within You*, you are now feeling significantly more confident and less nervous about writing your book. In this chapter, I will guide you to break through the emotions that arise as you are writing your book, including the frustration you might encounter with your computer or word-processing programs! It's my goal to have you be anything but defeated by the book writing experience so that you can fulfil your vision as an author. I reveal attitudes and perspectives you can adopt in order to become unstoppable as a writer. It will empower you to get back up when you fall down and provide coaching from my heart straight to yours that will encourage you to keep putting one foot in front of one another. My intention is to equip you with an effective mindset for bringing your book to completion, all the way from the moment you open the blank word document to the time you hold the book in your hands for the very first time.

Harnessing Persistence, Generating Momentum

There are many moments on your journey of writing book where you may want to give up and walk away. Just for the fun of it, let's list them out:

- Before you even begin (People do it all too often)

- When trying to find a title for the book

- In choosing what cover to have and how to get it designed

- Working out the outline and structure (often the hardest part)

- Mid-sentence or paragraph because you got tangled in your own words

- Part-way through because the book feels like it will take forever

- Near the end thinking, "Who cares about this anyway?"

- Not knowing how to publish the manuscript once you've finished

I'm sure you could add more. Even if your book took just a few days or weeks to write, the publishing process may test your patience. As well as equipping yourself with practical solutions to each of the problems you might face along the way (many of which I have addressed in this book), it will serve you to develop persistence: the essential key to overcoming all of them. Having persistence to push through and finish your book is sometimes as simple as saying to yourself, "GO, GO, GO! YOU CAN DO IT!" which I have done many times (and as silly as it sounds, it helps). And, at other times, motivation and encouragement isn't enough to generate the persistence you need to keep at it. Here are a handful of ways to tap into the inspiration you need for the next leg of the journey:

1. Reflect on Your Vision: Go Within

In Chapter 3, we talked about your vision as an author. Now (the moment you're struggling) is the time to remind yourself of your vision. Remind yourself of your end outcome. See the book in your hands. Think about how the book will benefit you professionally, financially and personally. Heartfelt, powerful visions have energy within them you can access anytime you need to.

2. Get Your Book Cover Designed

I am now in the practice of getting the cover for each book designed early on: even in the first weeks of writing my book. Once my cover is designed, I have certainty that the book will get finished. I print the full spread of the cover out (front, back and spine) and stick it to my wall where I can see it. You can do this to inspire yourself along the way.

3. Share Your Journey with People

You may be someone who thrives off social interaction. If you are (like me), then I suggest sharing your writing journey online through social media or in conversations with people. Tell them where you are up to. Post your book cover online. Share when you are writing. Go on a writing retreat and immerse yourself in a journey alongside other people. I love social interaction and I know that it assists me to stay focused on who I'm writing it for. It also inspires me to finish the book ASAP, so people can read it.

4. Think About the Readers

This follows on from social interaction. Focus on your readers; feel their presence while you're writing. Imagine them holding your book in their hands. Understand that you are providing them a service by writing your book. You will help them to solve problems, learn and grow, and become all they can be. Let it inspire you.

During the writing of this book, someone asked me whether lacking momentum is just a sign that the book isn't the right one or whether it's in our nature to avoid challenge. My simple answer to this is to ask your intuition. You only have to stop and be present with yourself for a moment to know whether the book you're currently working on is the one that you want to finish. I have worked on a handful of book ideas that never saw the light of day. In each case, I had to be willing to admit to myself that this book wasn't the one: and let go of it. Every single time you let go of an idea, two things will happen: one, a better idea will appear, or two, the same idea will keep coming back to let you know it was the one to carry through to the finish. So, simply ask yourself and then trust your answer. Put aside fears that there isn't a great book idea for you: there is. I promise you. They often come out of nowhere in an unexpected moment. I've had many clients tell me that the book 'demanded' to be written and the persistence that follows this is often unparalleled. You can have that too. You are only going to persist on outcomes that are truly important to you; and when you can't wait to write your book, the writing spirit will work through you.

If you are sitting at your computer feeling stuck and yet you know this book is 'the one', then may I encourage you to simply push yourself mentally. Identify your problem and what you are unclear on and work through it, so you can move on. Don't allow yourself to be too easily distracted or for very long. You want this goal. I view having mental persistence like lifting weights at the gym. The final reps in any set are the toughest ones. They hurt the most. You think, "There's no way I'll lift this," and then you summon your strength and you lift it. You know that if you walk away, you won't get the result. Book writing is the same. Harness that same determination and push through it. What's on the other side of that obstacle is pure magic: a moment where it all suddenly makes sense and the content 'clicks' together. It's incredibly satisfying. I don't even need to tell you how fulfilling having the book in your actual hands is, because I'm sure you have already thought about it a million times.

When you are stuck for ideas on content, work on other parts of the book. Tweak your introduction. Write your acknowledgements. Review your already-written chapters. Every bit of work you do counts; every word counts. Your patience and persistence will be your greatest assets on the journey.

See the Book and Your Life as One

This concept inspires me because it is one of the biggest points of difference between those who finish their books and the people who don't get their books done. I see every book as a part of both me and my life. And, because of this, I see every day as an opportunity to find ideas and content. Now, for this book, it's easy for me to draw content from my life for the manuscript as my days are focused on helping people to write and I teach topics in this book regularly. But, the same principle applied for my previous books. I could meet someone at a networking event and suddenly have an idea for a piece about spirituality. I could walk past someone in the street and get inspired for a chapter. I could pick up profound business principles to share, from the most seemingly insignificant moment.

There are opportunities for content for you everywhere if you're open to it and if you see your book and your life as one. Your life is packed full of ideas. It's around us every day, everywhere that we go. Whether we tap into it comes down to our attitude. When you are on a mission, you focus on what is important to you. You see it everywhere in the world. And, since you are writing about what is important to you, your life becomes a continual muse for your book. For example, you might be writing a book about raising an amazing family. And every day, you watch your own children grow. Every day, they bring you insights and realizations that you can share with your readers. The same applies for growing a business and writing a book about entrepreneurship.

The blessing of seeing your book and life as one is that the content you write that was inspired by your life is likely to be original: fresh, real, raw and hot off the press. It may even be content that you hadn't thought about when you first began writing. Like I once said in a live training, "There is a book inside every chapter of your life." Ask yourself in daily life:

What can I write about from this?

Is there something valuable here I can bring to my readers?

Every day of your life is research for your book. I adore the concept that a writer is always working, because they are either writing or thinking (or dreaming) about writing, as though life is an intermission between the words. So, see the words and your life as one and make them both magnificent. Let the book enhance your life and your life enhance your book.

Heart-Opening Moments

In order to inspire you further, I'm going to share with you a series of the heart-opening moments I have experienced in publishing my books so far. You will have many of these once you become an author, and I want to make sure that you know what is possible for how the book will transform your life even after you've finished writing it. Here is the first story.

In 2011, my book *Transformational Leaders* was published. Several months later, I attended a networking event one evening where a series of people knew me and knew of my book. Several of them had been given a copy or bought it for themselves. I delivered a short talk that night, and afterwards, a gentleman approached me and introduced himself. After telling me that he had enjoyed it (a nice accolade in itself), he then told me that him and his wife kept their copy of my book in the pocket on the back of the driver's seat in their family car. And then, he told me that his nine year-old daughter would frequently pick up the book and start making up her own story about how she was a transformational leader. Now I don't know about you, but that struck a chord with me: it was proof that our books can alter and influence future generations and give birth to leaders. My appreciation for the power of being a published author grew that night.

Fast-forward to 2013 when my fourth book, *The Inspirational Messenger*, emerged. I had gifted a copy to my mother to read (of course), and one morning while we were staying together, I poked my head into her bedroom to say good morning. I found her sitting up in bed, with tears running down her face – and my book open in her lap. My first thought was, 'Oh God, what have I done?' I asked her if she was okay and what was happening. It took her about 45 seconds to answer me. When she finally did, I too had tears running down my face. She said, "It feels like you're talking to my soul." Wow. Humbled. Since this was my intention with the book – to share my soul on paper – these words were music to my ears and my heart. Mission accomplished.

Another story which occurred around the release of *The Inspirational Messenger* was in early 2014. I was travelling through Melbourne and staying with one of my girlfriends for a few days on my way to Adelaide for business. While I was staying in her apartment, I had the opportunity to meet one of her friends. We got talking, sharing what we did for 'work', when the book came up in conversation. I happened to have a copy with me (advice: if you're traveling, take a handful of your books with you), and the girlfriend said that she wanted to read it and that she'd be staying in that night to do just that. Now, this might not mean much to you, but for me, it was an opportunity to experience first-hand that what I write can be meaningful enough to move someone to spend their Saturday evening reading it. I hope the same occurs for you as you become an author. These three stories are a handful of many, and a true testament to just what is possible once your book goes out into the world. Keep your heart and mind open to the potential.

Giving Up Is Not an Option... And Neither is Failure

Don't walk away from your book and don't you dare give up. I gave up on myself as a writer when I was 17 years old. I had received the idea while working as a receptionist at a gym and studying at University to write a book called *The Changes*. The book was to help people integrate the power of self-help into every day of their lives. Six months into writing what ended up being a 70,000 word manuscript, I read the book *The Power of Intention* by Wayne Dyer. When I read the book, I realized that one chapter in my book was similar to a chapter in his. I was crushed. In fact, I let it stop me from writing completely. I let it defeat me. To this day, I haven't added a word to the manuscript and it lives on in an incomplete state. Having said that, several people have read the rough manuscript and been blown away by my depth of understanding about the universe at large when I was only 18 – and if I'm honest, I have been, too. I think back to where I was in life – living out of home, studying full-time University, and working – and I'm humbled by what I wrote during that phase of my life. As it stands now, I have tentative plans to release the rough manuscript in honour of the young writer in me who so badly wanted to be help humanity but who gave up on herself before the book saw the light of day.

I won't ever forget that moment. It taught me to be original. It taught me to allow what is mine and the juicy content surface: content that only I could have generated and the wisdom only I could have gotten access to. You have this within you. You will know when you are writing it because you will feel it: that's all there is to it. That moment was a blessing in disguise, albeit one that took me years to find, and that is now invaluable to me. I now coach myself and every person I train to do the same thing: find their originality and stamp their name across it.

Now, here's the tough part: it took me nearly two years of my life to feel confident enough to pick up the pen again. I thought everything I had been living for was gone. I went through depression in those two years, which I believe is a direct result of the fact that I had given up on my greatest love: the written word. I still remember the day I began writing again. It was like someone put the colour back into the world. Once I found my footing, I was able to begin crafting my future as a writer, speaker, and now multiple-published author in the world.

I've given up on myself more than one time since then. Sometimes you don't know the wind was in your sails until it is knocked out completely. I have stood beside the likes of Elizabeth Gilbert, JK Rowling and Dan Brown and felt ashamed of the number of my book sales compared to theirs. I have thought, "Hey, maybe I'm just not as talented as they are." I know what that feels like to doubt yourself as a writer. It rips you apart. But, I also know what it feels like to have people write to me and say that my book changed their life. I know what it is like to have people thank me for the difference that the book made to them, and that because of it, they chose something more for themselves: which I believe in my heart, we are all worthy of.

These moments of failure can play an essential role. It is life's way of making sure that we have our hearts in the right place when we write. It's making sure that our hearts are even in it at all. And every time that we give up on words and get brought back to them, we pass the test that reveals the people who are serious about bringing great teachings, mystical writings, and phenomenal stories to this planet. Each of my books has made me both doubt and find myself a little. Each one has peeled back the layers to reveal the light that is inside of me. That is growth. Each book has taught me new things about myself, life and the world. And, each one has stirred me to ask deeper questions about what my strengths are as an author.

Giving up on your dream to be a writer is painful. It's sometimes worse than losing a lover. It runs deeper than your relationship with people, because it comes back to your relationship with you. Giving up on your writing is like giving up on yourself. It's like saying that what you have to say, and more importantly, what you want to say, isn't valuable. It's like saying "Oh well" to your dream when you trip and stumble. You could only give up right before your dream was about to come true. In that moment, you can write it off and stuff the pain down inside you. Or, you can face it, feel it, and thank God that you care enough to feel anything at all. Then, pray to the heavens for the guidance you need to put you back on your feet, so you can finish this book that the world needs. It will come every time if you are open to it.

Nurturing the Creative Spirit

These are my top eight suggestions for nurturing your creative spirit:

1. **Reflect on how far you've come** – Focus on your achievements to date. Focus on what you have done well. Build upon it.

2. **Receive coaching or encouragement** – Engage a writing coach or book mentor to work with you. They will (if they know what they're doing) encourage you and guide you to focus forwards and highlight your strengths.

3. **SAVE your work** – There is nothing worse than losing your writing because you didn't save it. Get in the habit of saving your work! Send your updated manuscript to yourself via email for safe-keeping at the end of every writing session.

4. **Try your hand at different styles of writing** – By trying new types of writing, you might stumble across a style you're great at that you weren't aware of before.

5. **Break your book down into smaller goals** – Divide your big goal (the whole book) into many goals (individual chapters and sections) and tick them off as you go. This will give you the feeling of progress as you work on your book.

6. **Celebrate your milestones** – Every single moment in the book writing process is worth celebrating. So, celebrate them. Every word written is one less to go.

7. **Share your journey** – Connect with other budding authors or people who believe in you as you are writing. Find a community of writers to join. Keep them informed. Update them about your progress.

8. **Give yourself pep talks** – You can build up strength and persistence through continually encouraging yourself as you write. It shows yourself that you are here for the long run and believe in yourself.

Make a commitment to yourself that you will write this book and see it through: no matter what happens and no matter how long it will take you. There will be times when you doubt yourself and times when you think it will never be finished, but again, you must go back to the reason why you felt compelled to begin the journey in the first place. Draw on the inspiration that is all around you. Keep nurturing your mindset. Coach yourself and be coached by experts. You will learn things about yourself along the way – things of great value – and you will realise that you owe it to the world to unleash your talent. You will thank yourself for it and people will appreciate it.

Chapter 12: Titles, Subtitles, Covers and More

"People say don't judge a book by its cover, but unfortunately, we all do."

Emily Gowor

*I*n this chapter, you will learn what how to prepare your book to succeed, go the furthest, and be what you consider as a great achievement. You could say that this chapter will show you how to 'dress your book for success', which is the art of ensuring that your book is inspiring on the inside and out. A well-dressed book is a book which:

- Is visually appealing

- Draws the reader in, even from a distance

- Is visually unique and different from other books

The advantage of dressing a book properly start with increasing the likelihood of both attracting and securing media attention. Once you are published, you may want to be featured on radio and television shows, in newspapers and magazines, in online podcasts and blogs, and so on. Having a book that looks great and is well positioned is going to assist with this. When you are choosing the design elements and appearance of your book, it's important to consider where your book might appear. Give yourself permission to think big.

People *will* see your book – even if you only intend to sell a few hundred copies – so prepare it to be seen by millions. Aim high and work backwards. You want your book to be a book that you can hold up, talk about in front of crowds, and be proud of. You want the appearance, title and so on, of your book to inspire people. All of the elements we are about to cover in this chapter will, when done well, increase your sales and capture the attention of potential and future readers. It will turn your book into a "You have to read this" kind of book.

When your book looks and feels beautiful and reads exceptionally well, you will feel satisfied. Dressing your book for success means paying attention the finer details and not stopping until you are 100% content with what is before you release it to the world. I can't stress the content in this chapter enough, as it all contributes to your book having what I call 'sell-appeal'. Sell-appeal is where people are automatically intrigued by your book. Every single book is a small (or big) brand within and of itself. Because of this, it's important that you consider the launch of the book you are writing as the launch of the next level of your business. It is going to assist you to achieve the next level of your professional pursuits. This book will create a culture around itself and, whether you like it or not, people will associate you with how it looks... enough said!

The remaining pages in this chapter will coach you step-by-step on how to create 'sell-appeal' to your book. Let's begin with the title and subtitle of your book, as they are crucial and go hand-in-hand with many of the several components that follow it.

Book Title & Subtitle

The reason I address book titles first is because it is difficult to get your cover designed unless you have a title. Of course, it also makes it hard to start telling people about the book you are working on if you don't know what it is called. When coaching people on how to create a title and subtitle for their book, I begin by explaining the purpose of a title. In a nutshell, the purpose of the title of your book is to a) tell the reader what the book is about, b) invoke the readers' curiosity. As we explored in Chapter 2, people will pick up a book off the shelf in a bookstore based on the title alone, and so it's not hard to understand the crucial nature of a title that works.

The main title of your book is often the pin-point for all of the attention. Now, it's common for fiction novels and a handful of other genres to leave out a subtitle completely. If you are writing a fiction book, then you might consider doing this. However, a vast majority of books take advantage of the extra real estate on the cover of their book by including a subtitle too. A general rule to keep in mind when creating titles and subtitles is what I refer to as a subjective vs. objective balance. What this means is that either your title or your subtitle will be subjective: it will invoke curiosity and intrigue the reader. It might even become like a tagline or culture (I'll give you an example in a moment). The subjective component of the overall title won't necessarily tell the reader exactly what the book is about: it is emotive and stirs the reader to think about what the book is about. The subjective component of the title might even pose a deep question. It can be a little abstract and even surreal, but definitely intriguing.

On the flip side, the objective element of a book title has the simple purpose of telling the reader what the book is about. There is nothing worse than picking up a book where the title and subtitle give you absolutely no clue what the book is about. Remember back to *The Book Pyramid* for a moment: you will recall that the title and subtitle (positioned right up the top) have the purpose of communicating the main message of the book. This applies here. So, the objective part of your title is the factual piece. It should tell your reader what the book is about in a catchy and thought-provoking way. The factual part of your title will talk to the people who are your ideal readers: it's your way of letting them know that this book is for them.

Let me give you some examples of titles to explain this for you. I'll do this by taking a handful of books that use both title and subtitle and breaking it down for you.

Example 1) *The 4-Hour Work Week: Escape 9-5, Live Anywhere and Join the New Rich* by Timothy Ferriss

In this example, the title is more on the subjective side as it invokes curiosity and intrigue. It moves the reader to ask, "What is the four hour work week?" and inspires them to dream about what a four-hour work week might look like for them. On the other hand, the subtitle tells you exactly what the book is about and communicates what the outcome for you as the reader is. Notice here that the book sells a desirable outcome to the reader: it touches on a desire that is felt by millions of people in the USA, Australia, New Zealand and more, which is partly why this book became a New York Times Best-Seller.

Example 2) *The Values Factor: The Secret to Creating an Inspired and Fulfilling Life* by Dr. John Demartini

With Dr. John Demartini's book, *The Values Factor*, the title is the subjective component. It makes you wonder what 'the values factor' is. It then follows on to explain what the book is about in the subtitle. It's clear by reading the title that this book will help you to live a more meaningful life – one that you love – and it promises (through the title) to help the reader tap into the 'values factor' for themselves.

Example 3) *The Outsiders Edge: The Making of Self-Made Billionaires* by Brent D Taylor

In Brent D. Taylor's book, *The Outsiders Edge*, the title is subjective component. The subtitle of the book explains what the book is about: the making of self-made billionaires. The book intrigues the reader to know what the outsiders' edge is (since billionaires are a minority in this world) and to learn more about how each of the billionaires literally made their own success. Again, the book catches the attention of the reader while also telling them what the book is about.

Now, is it possible that your title and subtitle won't be in direct contrast between objective and subjective? Absolutely. An example of this might be the book by one of my previous clients, Lynn Hope Thomas: *Breaking Through Loss: One Powerful Story, One Scientific Method*, where the subtitle and the title are a blend of both. This is fine; so long as you don't move too far to one extreme and lose (or bore) the reader. To wrap up this lesson, let me give you some examples of book titles that are either too far on the subjective side or in reverse, too far on the objective side. Please note: all of these have been made up to demonstrate the point.

All Subjective, No Objective	All Objective, No Subjective
A Wanderers Journey: The Dark Night of My Soul	Refrigeration: How to Fix Your Fridge
The Butterfly: When God Breathed Air Under Her Wings	How to Dig Holes: Finding the Best Shovel
Blue: How I Felt	The International Reference Book of Medicine: A Scientific Guide to Understanding Disease

Take a moment now to pick up five books around you and identify which one is which in their title. Is one more subjective and the other objective? Do the titles make sense? Is there something missing from their titles? Observe which titles appeal to you and which ones don't. And now, take a moment to identify why it did or didn't appeal to you. Is the title too fluffy? Is it too boring? Too factual? Unclear? Train yourself to notice great titles and also titles that are weaker and use them as guide for choosing your own. Let's explore it the components of a great book title.

The Components of a Great Book Title

1. Clear

The first component of a great book title is that it must be clear. In other words, it has to make sense. It's important that your title doesn't confuse your reader. They need to understand what the book is about when they read it, so I don't suggest being overly cryptic.

2. Unique

The second component is that your title is unique. I don't recommend creating a title that is a play on famous books like The Secret or Rich Dad, Poor Dad. Books that sound too much like another famous title often don't stand out and readers (and people in general) can get the sensation that you aren't creative enough to do something different. There are an infinite number of combinations of words in this world – more than anyone could ever count – so create a title that is unique and catchy. There is a perfect title for your book that is unique and that accurately represents the main message of the book.

3. Sexy

The third component of a great title is that it is sexy. What I mean by this is that when you say it out loud people respond with, "Oh! I like it!". The book Think and Grow Rich has a punchy and intriguing title. You ideally want a title that looks good on your cover and sounds appealing to the reader.

4. Curiosity

The fourth component of a great title is that it creates curiosity for the reader. It must grab their attention and make them want to know more about the topic of the book. This can be achieved through either your title or subtitle: or both.

Besides these four core components of a great book title and subtitle, you can also consider the following when choosing a title:

- A book title/subtitle shouldn't be too long. Either your title or subtitle should be shorter than the other one. It needs to be easy to say, for you and readers.

- Is the title catchy enough?

- Does the title tell the reader what the book is about?

- Does the title match the internal content of the book?

- Will the title challenge people or create controversy?

- Does the title talk about the outcome the reader will get from the book?

You can have fun creating the title for your book. It's too easy to become overly concerned with whether your title is 'right'. Whenever I am creating a title for a book, I put aside all concerns about whether the title is right or wrong and place my attention on finding the title that sits right with the author (whether it's me personally or a client) and that matches the book the best. Try to see the title-creation stage of becoming an author as an exploration as opposed to a chore. Bring your creative mind to the table and be open to possibility. Giving your book a title is like naming a child: it gives it a spirit of its own. And, titling your book is also a powerful stage in the book writing process where you bring the idea to life, as it will capture, express and reflect the core message of the book and your message for the world.

Producing Your Book Title

For some of you, the title of your book will make itself known before you start writing. In fact, it may be your primary inspiration for writing the book. I have experienced this where it is because of the title that I want to write the book in the first place. But, for other people, the title will come when they are further along in the writing process. Both are fine. There are no set rules on it. The title for *The Inspirational Messenger* came to me two months before I contemplated writing a book. And, the title for this book, *The Book Within You*, came out of my mouth in conversation the morning after I became clear that this would be my next book. If your title has come to you already, great. If it hasn't, don't worry. I'm about to show you two different but effective approaches that you use to can 'find' the perfect title for your book. Read on – and then choose the one that feels right.

1. Title Creation

The first approach for creating your book title is to work it out. It requires you to think. It requires you to enter your creative zone. If you're working your title out through persistence, you might be digging through average book titles in order to find the right one. Because of this, it might require patience and TLC to get it right. Or, it might happen quickly. It depends on how clear the book you are writing is. If you are following the 'work-it-out' approach, it can also help to think logically about what a great title for the book would be. Here are two different ways you can "work out" your title:

   a) Mind-Mapping

The first approach is through mind mapping, where you sit down with a blank piece of paper and some pens. Then, ask yourself, "What is the core message of the book?" As you focus on it, write out all the words you can think of that relate to the book on a mind-map. It also helps to write out key phrases that might be included in the title. You will quickly see which words are stronger than others for your title and be able to rule out the ones that don't work. By using this approach, you will often find that the title appears in the midst of the words.

Play with different combinations of the words and phrases that are on the page. Say them out loud. Separate them into your title and subtitle and ask which one belongs where. Persist through trial and error until you find the one that 'clicks'. You will know when you have found it because it will sound and feel right.

   b) Market Feedback

The next approach is to do market feedback. This is where you can ask other people what they think a good a title for your book would be. This includes getting input from, friends, fans, customers, and so on. You can use one, many, all or a combination of these people to perfect your title. One thing to note here if you are using market feedback is to realize that they may or may not be the best title based on whether they would personally buy and read the book. It's because of this that I suggest using other people's opinions as input, not a rule. Always keep your own book and future as an author above other people's opinion. I want you to stand in your power: speak up for the title that is right and don't stop until you know it is the one.

Let's move on to the second approach to creating the title for your book.

2. "Receiving" Your Title

Title creation option number two is the opposite to approach number one. It is simply to allow the title to come to you. This could be considered as a spiritual approach where you let go and allow the title to pop into your head at the perfect moment. It involves less thinking and more feeling. You don't push or force the title to appear. You simply feel into your book – focusing on the essence of it – and allow the title to just come to you. It might appear through a random thought. You might see part of the title on a billboard. You might hear or see it during a meditation. You might wake up with it in your mind one morning. Or, it might come out of your mouth during conversation with. I will say here, that talking about your book with someone can be a great way to 'find' the title.

What Do I Do Now?

Once you have worked decided on the title for you book, I want you to do one important thing for me: register the URL for the title. If you can, I suggest owning the space on the web for your book. You will need this URL to develop your sales page for the book later down the line, which will be useful for pre-sales before you publish and for promotion once the book is released. It makes it easier to send people to a direct website which is the title of your book as opposed to telling them to go the 'Shop' on your personal website. If you can't secure the direct URL for your book because it is on back order or has already been taken, I suggest using a variation of it that doesn't change the title of the book e.g. www.theinspirationalmessengerbook.com.

The Book Cover

Your book cover is the next crucial component of creating a book that impresses potential readers. The cover is way to communicate to your potential readers. It tells the reader about you and what the book has to offer for them. This especially applies when there is no personal contact with the reader besides the book cover, e.g. the reader walking into a bookstore and seeing your book. Let's run through the main criteria for a powerful book cover, remembering that while people say don't judge a book by its cover, we all do.

1. It represents you well as the author

2. It represents the message accurately

3. It represents your business (and what you are promoting) well

4. It is eye-catching and attractive

5. It uses the right colours

6. It matches the inside of the book (in style and feel)

7. It is a clean design where design elements are integrated

8. It is consistent between the front, back and spine of the book

9. It makes sense – e.g. it isn't confusing

10. It matches the genre of the book

It's essential that you keep your standards high and that you love your book cover. If you aren't comfortable with the cover of your book, you will feel uncomfortable showing people and promoting it, which will, in turn, limit your book sales.

"Where Do I Get My Cover Designed?"

- There are a handful of options for how to get your book cover designed. The first one is to work with one graphic designer until you have the design that you want. If you are doing this, you need to be clear on what you want before you work with the designer. Otherwise, you will play a game of hit and miss until you hopefully wind up with an amazing cover. The other option which I recommend to my clients it to use a website called *99 Designs* (www.99designs.com). *99 Designs* is an online graphic design company that sources designers from all over the world to work for clients to produce everything from logos to business cards to magazine and book covers. Here's how it works for getting a book cover designed:

- You pay a one-off upfront fee for your chosen design contest

- You create a design brief detailing your book cover (with as much information as possible)

- The design brief is posted online. Designers from all over the world submit designs to your design contest (with the intention of producing the winning design)

- You give feedback on designs to receive improvements and further designs, selecting which designs you like best and working with your favourite designers

- You move through the initial, qualifying and final rounds until you have a design

The entire contest typically takes 7-10 days from the start to the finish (where you have the design files for your book cover). A standard contest can attract anywhere from 50 to 200 designs or more depending on the complexity of your design and it is a great way to explore new possibilities for the cover of your book. *99 Designs* enables the user (you) to work with the creativity of several designers as opposed to just one designer. This often means you wind up with a better design than what you originally intended when you began. Over the duration of the contest, authors who have used 99 Designs find that they become clearer on what they want their final cover to be and often move on from their original idea to something greater. I have used 99 Designs several times for cover design, each time resulting in a quality outcome. Covers I have designed through the contests include the covers for *The Unlikely Entrepreneur, The Inspirational Messenger* and *The Book Within You*. I look forward to seeing your cover design soon.

It's important that your book cover resonates strongly with you as the author. I believe it's important to love your cover as much as you love the content of your book. When you look at your book, I want you to feel inspired to share it with the world and show everyone you know. Ask yourself the following questions when you are musing over what your perfect cover will be:

What are the main symbols that represent the book?

Which images remind me of the book?

What icons match or capture the inside of the book?

Which colours resonates with the theme of the book?

And finally,

What would I ultimately love my book cover to look like?

Create a list of items in response to these questions and begin to imagine (or even sketch) what the perfect cover for your book might be.

When the Cover Shows Its Face

I often find with aspiring authors (and also with my own books) that once the plan and title of the book are clear, a vision for the cover appears. When you are truly present with what the book is about – whether that is business, sales, leadership, relationships, health, spirituality and so on – and clear on your message and angle on that topic, knowing what the cover is becomes easy.

When I first began writing *The Inspirational Messenger* over the 2013 Easter weekend, I was wondering what the cover would be. I had an intuition that the cover of the book was going to be white, but that was all I knew. As I continued writing, I closed my eyes and imagined the cover. I saw something appear in the centre of the front cover, although I couldn't make out what it was. The next day, I thought about the cover again and I saw that the icon in the middle of the cover was blue. I didn't know what the object was, but I knew it was blue. By the time I had nearly finished writing the book (over my four day marathon), it suddenly came to me that the image in the centre of the white cover was a blue feather.

I felt inspired. I logged onto Google and looked up the meaning of a blue feather. I soon discovered that the feather has long been known as a symbol of wisdom and bringing celestial messages from the spiritual world into the human world. Of course, with a title like *The Inspirational Messenger*, this imagery was perfect for the book. I had goose bumps all over me when I read the meaning online. I then had the cover designed to match the vision. Let this story inspire to trust that the perfect cover will come to you. In the meantime, place your attention on the content between the covers and mastering an amazing book.

Chapter & Sub-Chapter Titles

The titles of the chapters and sub-chapters in your book are as important as the title of the book itself. These titles play two roles in your book. They:

1. 'Sell' the buyer by catching their attention and creating intrigue

2. Close the 'gaps' in your manuscript

Remember now to the earlier chapters in the book when we spoke about what it is that makes people buy books. One of those components related to the TOC (Table of Contents) and how people will do the 'flick-through' when standing in a book store or at the back of the room in an event. Well, the headings of your chapters and sub-chapters will stand out during the flick-through. So, it makes sense to ensure that these titles – both chapter and sub-chapter – are intriguing and interesting. The title of the book is the first hook and each chapter and sub-chapter title confirm to the reader that the book is worth buying.

The second purpose of the chapter and sub-chapter titles is to close the gaps in your manuscript. When the reader comes to the end of a paragraph or sentence and reads an interesting, captivating sub-chapter title, it naturally creates the desire to read on. This minimizes the chances of them putting your book down. The titles inside your book don't have to be the wittiest titles to intrigue the reader: it all depends on the genre and content in your book. Here are some examples of chapter and sub-chapter headings that may give you food for thought when creating your own. These have been selected from my own books and client manuscripts:

- What Happens When You Flick the Inner Switch

- The Essential How-To of Relationships

- Help! My Confidence Is on The Loose!

- Belief = Achievement

- A Method to The Madness

It is important to make sure that the headings of the chapters and sub-chapters in your book give the reader some idea of the content that is about to come and that they make sense grammatically. Think about the content that is in the chapter or sub-chapter before you choose the heading for that section in the book. I also suggest ensuring there is a consistency in the style of these titles throughout the book to give the reader a stronger sense of the core message and theme of the book.

About the Author

Let's bring our attention now to an essential component of becoming an author which can be overlooked in the hurry to get your book into print: The About the Author section. The About the Author aspect of your book (which includes the interior as well as what is shown on the cover) includes two core elements:

1. Your Author Bio

2. Your Author Photo/Headshot

Let's start with your author bio. Your author bio is actually not one, but two bios: a long and a short version. The longer version of your bio appears at the end of your manuscript (inside the book) after the Conclusion and Acknowledgments. This author bio is around 250-300 words in length and features your headshot alongside it. In an ideal world, your bio would fit onto a single page within your book, so keep this in mind when you are writing the bio as it may need to be shortened or lengthened to fit the page size of your book. Although some people do include an author bio in their book that extends over two pages, I generally don't recommend it as it tends to look messy. If you want to tell the readers everything about you, add your website addresses at the bottom of the page.

The short version of your bio is no more than two short and concise sentences long and it appears on the back cover of your book. It is a brief snapshot of you who you are and what you do. It may read something like:

> Emily Gowor is a multiple published author and speaker
> devoted to bringing books and inspiration to the world.

That's it! The reader will be able to glean more insight about you when they read your long bio inside the book. This bio may be more challenging to write. I suggest you pick up a series of other books and flick to the back cover to assist you. It doesn't have to be fancy, it just needs to get the point across.

Let's move on to your author headshot. Your author headshot is sometimes displayed on the back cover of your book next to the short author bio and, more commonly, inside the book beside the long version of your author bio. Here are my tips on how to get a great headshot for yourself as an author (which of course, you can also use in your online brand, on your website and in other locations throughout your business):

- Get a professional photo shoot done: the quality will be worth the investment!

- Utilize the same headshot on the back cover as you do with your bio on the inside of the book: it creates consistency

- Wear colours that suit you: it will help you shine and stand out

- Choose clothes that help you to 'speak' to your target readers and that compliment your desired public image

- For women: wear an appropriate amount of make-up. Don't go overboard: this is business, not a modelling shoot!

- Lift your chin up and smile: it will help you to appear approachable and warm

- Stand or sit with good posture: this will help to create a clean portrait

- Full body may not be the best option for your author photo (hence the phrase headshot)

Work on your author bio and headshot until you are satisfied they represent you well. Remember: you are creating a public image for yourself by becoming an author, and if you're going to create one, you want to create one that you love. It will take you a long way when it comes to attracting (and securing) new opportunities.

The Blurb

Let's explore what the secret to a powerful blurb is and how to write one. It's true that there is an art to producing a great blurb and that some people simply have a knack for writing book descriptions that really sell the book. But if you are new to the task, here are some pointers to help you create the blurb for your book:

- **Write out the 3-5 main points that need to be communicated about your book**

  E.g. Teaches the reader how to triple the sales in their business, coaches the reader to find a deeper sense of spirituality, answers the life-long question about what our purpose on Earth is.

- **Identify the 'sound-bites' or core phrases that you will use to describe your book**

  E.g. "An inspirational guide to business", "A meaningful and profound read", "A truly heartfelt book that reveals..." or "Packed with content that will help you to..."

- **List out the top 5 words you would use to describe the nature of the content in your book**

  E.g. Inspirational, powerful, awakening, empowering, educational, informative, heart-opening, heart-warming, brilliant, meaningful, raw.

- **Review other book blurbs for inspiration – and then write yours**

Your blurb is likely to be somewhere between 200-250 words, depending on the size of your book and how much text you want to display on the back cover. I suggest writing an initial draft without trying to get it perfect. Then work on tweaking, improving and finalizing it. The content of your blurb is likely to become clearer the more content you add to the manuscript as your clarity about what the book is about (grows. As you write the blurb, remember that the two core purposes are:

1. To tell the reader what the book is about

2. To engage the reader enough to buy the book

You might choose to read your blurb to a select group of people and ask for their feedback. Remember, the blurb must accurately represent and sell the content in the book.

The process of designing, writing and creating the above elements of your book can be an exciting process. If you do become frustrated with any of them, walk away and come back to them with a fresh mind. Don't be afraid to consult a professional or to ask other people for their viewpoints, considering who they are and what their experience is before you do. Work through each component – the cover, the title, and so on – until you are inspired by them. Once the book is written, you will not only be fulfilled and inspired by the book, but you will be ready to release it to the people who are eager to read it.

Chapter 13: FAQ's

he final chapter of *The Book Within You* follows a similar fashion to the final sessions of my book writing trainings. Before closing off the training, I like to allow participants to ask any question they want in an open session, to ensure they receive the maximum value. I am often asked questions that I haven't answered before and everyone benefits from it. And so, Chapter 13, is a compilation of the most frequently asked questions from these sessions. Although not all questions and their answers will apply directly to you, they may benefit you in the future, so read closely.

How do I know when my book is finished?

Writing a book can feel like a never-ending process. By now, it's likely that you are already experiencing this for yourself. You can keep editing, tweaking, changing and rewriting. You can keep on adding content, well, forever. The final stages of producing a manuscript are a great opportunity for the perfectionist in all of us to come out and run rampant through the pages. So, how do you know when your book is actually complete, to the point where it's ready to enter final production? Here are four key indicators:

a) All the content in the book is written

b) The book flows well from start to finish

c) The 'extra' pieces to the book are written e.g. Introduction, Acknowledgments

d) You are 100% satisfied with the content: both what it is and how it has been written

Check over all four of these in your book and then decide at what point you will declare you book complete and ready for the next stage, bearing in mind that if you keep tweaking, you may never publish it! Give yourself a time frame in which to make all final changes... and then let it go.

How and when do I get endorsements for my book?

Endorsements build social proof around your book. They let potential readers know that other people have enjoyed and recommend it. In simple terms, it is a testimonial about the book. You can start collecting endorsements during the review and edit stages of your book. Once you have the testimonials there are a number of places you can use your endorsement, including the book sales page, email marketing, other marketing materials, social media and, of course, in the book itself (typically in the front before or after the title page). There are five steps to follow to when getting endorsements for your book. They are:

1. Who

Who would you love to give you a review of your book? Think beyond family, friends and clients. Think to your extended networks. It is okay to ask someone who you don't know to review your book. Think about whose endorsements would benefit you and your book the most. Write a list of their names.

2. Prepare Yourself

The next step is to prepare yourself before asking for testimonials and to be clear on what you are going to say when you write or talk to them. You are asking them if they would be willing to read your book and produce a 2-6 line review for your book. I personally think it is wise to let the person know that you would be honoured to have their name in the book: compliments will take you a long way. Let them know that it's important to you and that you have specifically chosen them for the endorsement.

3. Approach the Person

You now need to contact the person. One of the most challenging aspects about gathering endorsements can be managing timeframes to get the reviews in before your deadline to publish. Beware that high profile people usually have a busy schedule and you may need to allow up to even two months to receive their endorsement. This depends on how warm your relationship with them is. Bear in mind that some people may say, "Yes I would love to give you a testimonial" because they are being polite and then they may not do it. Confirm with them that they will do it and give them your deadline.

4. Refine the Endorsement

Once you have received the endorsements, you will many need to edit them as sometimes the grammar needs improving, or the review is too short or long for the book. Edit it and check it back with the person to have them sign off on it before you publish it.

5. Thank the Person

I suggest thanking each person and giving them a copy of your book as a sign of gratitude for them taking time to give you an endorsement. At the very least, send them an email expressing your appreciation for them helping you to promote the book.

It is up to you how many endorsements you collect. How many do you want to use in the book? Some books have two and some have twenty. I had a client who featured 20 pages in the front of the book; as you can tell, it was a marketing piece. As I said previously, you can gather endorsements as you are writing just as long as your book is complete enough to read.

What if I start my book and back out because I'm scared?

First of all, I would say fear is not necessarily a bad thing: it means that you are living on your edge. As a writer, to have a little bit of fear can be valuable because it makes you conscious of what you are doing. Whenever there is fear, there is also hope. Ask yourself what you are afraid of. For example, you might be afraid that your writing isn't good. If you are worried about the quality of your writing, this means you care about your message – and that's a gift. It also means that you care about your readers and how much they like your book: something a best-selling author focuses on. Secondly, there are these people called... what is it... yes, that's it – EDITORS! A skilled editor has a great capacity to work with even poorly-written content and turn it a great piece.

Until you identify your fear, it's time to move past it. In *The Unlikely Entrepreneur* I wrote about overcoming depression when I was 19 years old. It was a raw story. It's only a small part of the book that fills people in on where I began my journey. I was nervous about putting it in the book because it is so personal: I was talking about laying on the floor not wanting to live. When I published the book, I gave it to a friend who I had known for years. He sent me a text three days later that read: "Wow. I didn't know that about you." His respect and love for me and his appreciation for who I am a person grew that day. And all because I decided not to let my fear get the better of me. So...

Ask yourself what you are afraid of. Are you afraid of people seeing you? Fabulous! Welcome to 7 billion people on the planet! We all have this fear. When people are reading your book, they're interested in getting the message. They are not worrying about who you are or what your weaknesses are. Quantify with the fear is and give yourself a pep talk. Sometimes you need a good pat on the back to keep you going. Your responsibility as an author is to share yourself in a way that moves people. So, regardless of whether people love it or have feedback on it or hate it, everybody is going to get something from it. And if they read it, that's the whole point of it. Stay true to yourself and your vision every step of the way and you will be rewarded.

I want to use illustrations and graphics in my book. What should I know?

There are no rules about whether using visual components in your book is a good move or not. It's up to you and depends on the book. Visual components include illustrations, charts, tables, pop-out boxes, charts, and so on. "How-to" books typically utilize more visual components. You may choose to use images to demonstrate a point clearly, as some people are visual learners. A memoir may include photos to share the story. Note: your graphics and images must be 300dpi in resolution to print clearly.

Should I use my face on the front cover?

Whether to use a photograph of yourself on the front cover of your book is a complex topic which I can give you my thoughts on, but the final decision rests with you. As you know, I chose to use my face on the cover of this book, *The Book Within You*. I connected with the core purpose of the book before deciding about whether to a) feature my photo or b) use a pen and paper (or something along those lines). A small group of people did suggest showing icons related to writing, however I was aware that these people weren't great at branding and struggled to promote themselves: it pays to be conscious of who you take advice from. I walked into a bookstore to see how many people use their face on the cover. What I noticed was that almost every genre in a bookstore has around 20% of books where the author featured their face on the cover and those books are from the leaders in the industry. Given that *The Book Within You* was written as a profiling piece, my decision was easy.

It's important to work with a great photographer for your cover image. It's important that your brand and business are represented accurately through the image you use. Think about the impression you want to make on people. Be conscious of who your target readers and clients are. Choose your photo well and use it with purpose.

I wrote a book years ago but haven't finished it. How do I resurrect it?

Because the book has not been released, I don't consider it dead. It's merely about finishing it. Make sure you update it however, as if some time has passed, the content and message may have evolved. The beauty in revisiting a half-written manuscript from years ago is that you will be able to see it through fresh eyes and most likely, gain an appreciation for it. Just take the time to revisit and refresh it, finish it, and make sure that you love it by the time you release it.

I walked away halfway through writing a paragraph. How do I revisit and pick up where I left off?

My advice for a situation where you have to walk-away mid-writing is to quickly jot down a few shorthand notes about what you are about to write so that when you come back, you can jog your memory and get back into the writing flow easily.

How much is too much to spend on publishing?

How much you invest in publishing your book is depends on the option you choose for publishing, e.g. self-publishing or traditional publishing. There are nuts-and-bolts packages that sell for around $1,000 AUD (I wouldn't recommend this based on previous client stories) and then there are the high-end packages that can cost anywhere up to $40,000. I wouldn't personally recommend spending more than $10,000 on a publishing package (depending on how many copies of your book are included) and I wouldn't advise ending up with 1,000 books in your garage unless you have a robust marketing plan to sell them. It all depends on your budget and what you are willing to invest to bring your book to life.

How do I make it to the big-time as an author?

I can answer this question in one word: marketing. I encourage every author to be willing to market their book, as it is the gateway to reaching readers and customers. A lack of marketing is often the greatest cause of an author feeling that their book was a flop. Marketing your book is about constant exposure. It's about having the willingness to get out into the world and promote it. It will usually take time to sell 5,000 or 10,000 copies of your book, so see your journey as a marathon not a sprint.

How you market is up to you. It depends whether you engage a marketing expert to assist you or go it alone. You can look for co-promotion opportunities, third-party online shops and speaking events where you can feature your book for sale at the back of the room. You can use content from the book to grow your database. You may not be aiming for a best-seller status, but I still encourage you to do marketing. Develop a strategy. What networking are you going to do? What radio shows will you go on? How will you grow your online profile? Build your empire... and the book will sell itself.

How long should the book production process take – from start to finish?

The entire timeline from start (a blank page) to finish (the book in your hands) is dependent on the author and dependent on publishing. As the author, you control how long the writing of the book takes. Some people write theirs over years. Other people write it inside of two weeks. *The Book Within You* was approximately a four month journey of bringing the content together. The time frame also depends on the book you are writing. The book might be research-based so you need more of time. Or, it could be a series of interviews which might take a shorter amount of time.

You can drive as fast as you want to, or you can stretch it out as long as you want to. I wouldn't recommend longer that two years. Set your deadline and keep it realistic based on what you know you can do. How long the publishing process takes depends on the publishing option you choose and could range from 6 to 16 weeks.

What if the book I'm writing is controversial?

This question opens up a big topic for some people as the book they want to publish has the potential to challenge people – or event countries – and it will fall back on them as the author. How controversial your book is needs to be considered. What will the ramifications of your book be? What opposition, if any, will it create? What feedback are you likely to get? What would the media drill you about, if anything? View the message in your book in context of the country you live in and in context of the country you wish to promote it in.

Being controversial can also mean that some publishers won't want to stand behind it – but on the flip side, it can easily gain you a great deal of attention, which of course, will help book sales. You can position your message in a way that doesn't challenge people so much by softening it and introducing it as a possibility, not a definite opinion. Or, you can stand strong for the message and be willing to fight for it. The key is to simply be conscious of the ripple your book could create and be prepared to handle it. Watch morning television a couple of days a week and see how the featured authors handle the questions they get. Notice that most of them believe in themselves and their book. Write what you believe in and find the courage to stand for it.

This brings us near the end of *The Book Within You*. Before you read the conclusion, I encourage you to reflect on the past 15 chapters and recap what you have learned through the book. You can use the following questions and space provided to assist you.

How did you feel about writing a book before you read this book? How do you feel now?

_____

_____

_____

_____

_____

_____

_____

_____

What were the most powerful lessons you learned in the book?

_____

_____

_____

_____

_____

_____

_____

What have you begun to apply for yourself in writing your book?

_____

_____

_____

_____

_____

Write about any other insights you had during *The Book Within You*:

_____

_____

_____

_____

_____

_____

_____

_____

_____

_____

And now, let's move into the conclusion. Thank you for being with me on this journey.

The Published Author

"Books are for nothing but to inspire."

Ralph Waldo Emerson

*B*efore I began writing this book, I knew I had a great deal to share on the topic of becoming an author. And now, I am more convinced than ever that this is only the beginning. I am convinced that you have more knowledge, depth and wisdom than you realize within you. I am certain that a part of you wants to bring it out and write about it. I know without hesitation that the world can benefit from you doing this and that you can impact a great number of lives through your pursuit of writing one or many books. And, I know that by you writing your book, you will awaken to this and so much more.

Writing books unleashes our greatness and expresses our potential. It is a self-growth, life-empowerment and business-growth exercise. It is in the pages of your book that you may discover your original body of work. It is in the pages of your book that you may find the healing you have been seeking. It is in the pages of your book that you may finally see the truth in why that relationship ended, why that career didn't work out, or why you moved to the other side of the world to start a new life. It is in the pages of your book that you may experience how brilliant you are: how intelligent, smart, creative. You figure out what's important to you. You learn what you know as well as what you don't. You discover your strengths. While writing your book, it will become obvious to you that you are born to do something great in the world and that there is more to you than you thought. And, while writing your book, you may discover just how many more books are still within you.

Bitten by the Writing Bug

Many authors begin the process of writing a book feeling that just to finish one book would be a great achievement. The idea of managing to complete a manuscript and have it published appears so big in the beginning that they haven't often even conceived the idea that there might be more than one book within them waiting to come out. But, by the time they reach the last page, they have more often than not been bitten by the writing bug. The sensation of finishing the book almost instantly and automatically unlocks the overwhelming desire to do it all over again. It seems crazy when you haven't even finished your first book, but once you are standing in that position where the book is in your hands, it seems easy to ask:

What _else_ would I love to write?

I have worked with many authors who became published and then wanted to forge forwards almost immediately into a second book – or into a series. In fact, many of them discover this desire long before they have finished the first piece. It's as though writing a book is like climbing a mountain; when you reach the top of the first mountain, you can't help but want to climb to the top of the next to see what that view looks like. Regardless of whether you are a business-writer, a research author or a spiritually-influenced story-teller, it's hard to deny that writing a book is inspiring. It's meaningful to hold your own work in your hands and say, "I wrote that."

Regardless of how many books you write, it's important to be satisfied with your achievements. Allow your book to go where it is capable of going. Make it available to the people who need it the most. Be grateful for every book sale. Appreciate yourself for the hard work you put in behind the scenes to make the book a reality Continue to produce exceptional content that benefits the lives of others. Push yourself and ask for feedback from your readers. Find out what they most want to read from you.

The more you write, the more you reveal the real you. Ask yourself what genre you would love to work on next. Is it the same one as your first book or a new one? Ask yourself what message, what stories, and what content you would most love to bring into the world. Don't stop until you find them. Just keep on writing. The challenge and growth you experience as a writer will reward you in ways you can't imagine right now.

It's Time to Rise and Shine

There is no doubt that becoming a published author requires you to stand out. And, because of this, it also requires you to give yourself the full permission to shine. As much as I solve logical problems that hinder people from creating their book, what underlies it is a deep understanding and appreciation of just how many emotions can arise before, during and after the book is born. We all wear layers of some kind in our everyday life, whether it is a public image, an expectation that we're trying to live up to, or a metaphorical brick-wall. Is there anything wrong with this? No, of course not. But, in my short time on Earth so far, I've discovered that it's far more rewarding to drop the image and be authentic. I also believe that the best books –, the ones that go the distance and have readers raving – are ones written by authors who were willing to be themselves. This is what ultimately gives the readers (who are real people just like you) the best experience of you as an author.

What would happen if you dug deep into who you are and brought that message out into the pages of your book? What would happen if you wrote a book about a topic that deeply inspires you? Being real with yourself about what book you would love to produce will lead to a greater outcome: it will get you out of your own way and enable you to naturally see a bigger vision for yourself, the book and the world.

Becoming an author is not just about the book. See, you might think it's about your message (which it is), or that it's about the reader (which it is), but it is also about you. This is YOUR life that will be impacted once the book is released. This is YOUR future that it will play a role in shaping. These are YOUR readers, who read YOUR words. It is about unfolding your wings or realizing that you have them (metaphorically speaking). And, it is about the personal brand that you are establishing for yourself by publishing your book.

It takes strength to craft your book and brand from the outside-in as well as the inside-out. You have to engage your inner critic and deeply examine each component of your book and align it with your vision. You have to ask yourself if the language you have written with is the language your readers relate to and understand. You have to know what your vision is. It took me about a year from age 19 to consolidate what I wanted to do in my future. Every book I write is now an expression of that vision. And, it took me several more years and publishing a handful of books to begin to master a well-written, well-positioned book. It took a real-life, hands-on experience to learn how to look at my books objectively and critique them in such a way that would significantly improve the end result.

This might involve choosing the right cover, and not just the prettiest one but the one that suits and sells the book. It might involve improving your own writing to communicate more effectively. It might involve being willing to take a risk and share something about yourself in a published book that not even your closest friends know about you. It might involve learning how to design an effective pre-sales page or a launch and marketing campaign for the book. It might involve letting go of the title you have been holding onto so tightly and searching for a better one. Education on both practical and emotional levels is essential for helping you to craft yourself and your book into what you would love them to be and taking it far beyond what you originally imagined could or would be possible.

Invest in coaching, training, and mentoring to propel you forwards and guarantee that you get your outcome: because your business needs it, you want it, and the world desires it. And cultivate strength to handle the inevitable discouragement at times you will experience once published, from people not purchasing it to people picking up spelling mistakes in the pages. Some people will like it. Some people won't. Some people will have their life forever altered because of what you wrote. And it won't land with other people. Be strong. Don't shut down in the face of it and suppress your feelings. On the contrary, open up. Keep improving. Don't give up. Do whatever it takes to fulfil the vision in your mind.

You have the rest of your life ahead of you. So, start living it more fully than you have before. No matter where you are, there is somewhere for you to go, so why not go upwards and onwards? Begin to discover the depth that is contained in every single day and in every single moment of your life. Write it. Publish it. Share it. Step outside your comfort zone and connect with others; make life come to life for thousands of people. What about your mark on the world? What about that? What about that legacy, that dream inside your heart?

The Write Time Is Now

Don't wait until something adverse happens in your life to write. Don't wait for the tides to turn, for the people to please you, for the right moment to come… because it never will. The message inside you doesn't work on timers like that. It doesn't know what January 15th means, and it doesn't wait for the sky to be light blue before it decides that now is the right time to be written: to be spoken, to be shared. It doesn't wait for you to be awake; it wakes you up.

The most powerful experiences of writing aren't based in the world of time. They exist in a moment that can only be described as the present moment. They are when life stops, you stop ageing, you stop worrying about the grey hairs on your head, and the dollars in your bank account. You allow your heart and mind to connect with the magic that cannot be seen but that can be felt. The magic that brings words to life and dreams come true. The write time is now. Every day. Any day. All day. Just now.

It's time for you to write. It's time to open up and let the book within you come out. There is no fear, no reason to stop, no reason not to shine. There is no problem that cannot be solved. There is no rationale against your capacities as a writer that can ever outweigh the calling of the soul. Help is only a click of a button or a phone call away. And most importantly, let your soul lead you, your heart guide you, and your mind raise you up to the heights you know you are destined for. Go forth and write.

The Author's Credo

I am blessed to have this time in my life to work
on this book – my masterpiece.

I take satisfaction in the progress that I have made and that I will make today.

I believe in my book, the messages within it, and
the vision it will fulfil in the world.

I know that every word I write takes me closer to my end goal.

I do what I can to nurture my creative writing mindset.

I honour myself as the author.

I know that without me, this book would not be written
or come into existence. Therefore, I am valued.

I allow myself the energy and space to focus.

I give myself permission to open up fully and allow the words to flow out.

I trust myself to write and know that I write well.

I understand that every paragraph written is a paragraph finished.

I know that my team around me have my back
and therefore the book will be great.

I acknowledge myself for finally writing the book that is within me.

May the book within me, come out.

Acknowledgments

My gratitude for those involved in the creation of *The Book Within You* is unbounded. I would first love to thank Michael Spillane who, through asking the right question, inspired this as my next published book. Secondly, I would love to thank Lynn Hope Thomas for being the first person ever to request my services as a book mentor. Without you, I would never have fallen in love with book mentoring, nor found out that I had a gift for guiding people to write. Hundreds and now thousands of people have benefited because of you, your heart and your determination.

Thank you to all of the people who interviewed me to capture and create content for the book: Dan Fleishman, Samantha Riley, Maria Solano, Sandhya Porritt, Anfernee Chansamooth, Vincent Kellsey and Kane Minkus (for welcoming me to present on the Singapore Mastermind group). My gratitude is extended to Elizabeth Chelson and Benjilou Tacsanan for creating transcriptions I could work from. I would also love to thank Ronald M. Cruz of Cruzial Designs for designing the cover for the book.

Thank you to the people who supported me to write this book: Jamie Stenhouse, Rhi Butler, Poy TB, Juraj Benak, Suzanne Waldron, Tony Inman, Geoff Alexander and many more. You have accompanied me on the journey to bringing my fifth book to life and for that, I am thankful beyond words. I would love to thank myself for surrendering to the calling to write this book as without my desire to bring the book within me out, this book wouldn't be here to help you bring the book within you, out. And finally, a warm thank you to all of my eager readers who were hungry to devour the years of content in these pages and for those who have purchased a copy of the book: past, present and future. I write for you.

About the Author

Emily Gowor is a multiple-published author, writer and inspirational speaker. Emily overcame depression at age 19 to build a profound and thriving career bringing writing and inspiration to the world.

As the author of more than published books – including *The Search for Inspiration*, *The Book Within You*, *The Write State of Mind*, and *The Inspirational Messenger* – Emily produced an award-winning blog in 2010 and 2011, attracting thousands of readers online. Emily was an editor on Dr. John Demartini's international best-selling book *Inspired Destiny* in 2009 and shared the stage with Dr. Demartini in Melbourne, Australia (2015).

As a winner of the 2012 and 2014 Anthill 30under30 Young Entrepreneur Award, Emily has been featured in a range of media spreading her messages of inspiration. Emily has years of experience in coaching authors to bring their message to the page. Having made a significant difference in the lives of many around the world by age 30, Emily finds inspiration in the world around her as she continues to bring her brilliance and love for humanity to the forefront into all she does.

www.emilygowor.com

www.ingramcontent.com/pod-product-compliance
Lightning Source LLC
Chambersburg PA
CBHW060356220326
41598CB00023B/2935